D0089031

A New Owner's
Guide to
LABRADOR RETRIEVERS

JG-107

Title Page: The most popular dog breed today, the Labrador Retriever is handsome, intelligent and even tempered.

The Publisher wishes to acknowledge the following owners of the dogs in this book: Diane Ammerman, Brenda Beckage, Rich and Linda Bednarski, Sally Bell, Bob and Lin Besley, Pam Blankenship, Lori A. Brittle, Cedarhill Kennels, Sharon Celentano, Ellen Cottingham, Denise Evans, Mary Feazell, Wyndcall Kennels, Jim and Debbie Gardner, Stephen and Betty L. Graham, Nancy Horvath, Connie Howard, Marc Huff, Lori Kelsey, Hans and Lynn Koller, Mary Lou Lempert, Luanne Lindsey, Emily Magnani, Ted and Kathy Ted McCue, Michelle McGroarty, Diane Menard, Julie A. Meyers, Rob and Beverly Montgomery, Holly and Judy Niece, Sonya Ninneman, Elaine Perkins, Patricia Perriello, Joe and Kim Petkosh, Frank Purdy, Pete Russos, Jacquelin Savelli, Johanne Savoie, Diane L. Schlemmer, David W. Schnare, Martha Sheppard, Kathy Sneider, VMD, Nancy Stewart, Judith Strom, Buzz Taylor, ErnieValluraw.

Photographers: Mary Bloom, Paulette Braun, Mary Feazell, Isabelle Francais, Robert Pearcy, Vince Serbin, Ron Smith, Judith Strom, Karen Taylor.

The author acknowledges the contribution of Judy Iby for the following chapters: Sport of Purebred Dogs, Traveling with Your Dog, Identification and Finding the Lost Dog and Health Care.

ACKNOWLEDGMENTS

My sincere gratitude to Ann Sergi, American Kennel Club Library; Mary Knapp, Retriever Field Trial News; Vicky Creamer; Martha Sheppard; Luanne Lindsey; Nick Mickelson; Beverly and Rob Montgomery for all aid, especially sleuthing. My deer stalker hat is off to you.

© 1996 by T.F.H. Publications, Inc.

Distributed in the UNITED STATES to the Pet Trade by T.F.H. Publications, Inc., One T.F.H. Plaza, Neptune City, NJ 07753; distributed in the UNITED STATES to the Bookstore and Library Trade by National Book Network, Inc. 4720 Boston Way, Lanham MD 20706; in CANADA to the Pet Trade by H & L Pet Supplies Inc., 27 Kingston Crescent, Kitchener, Ontario N2B 2T6; Rolf C. Hagen Inc., 3225 Sartelon St. Laurent-Montreal Quebec H4R 1E8; in CANADA to the Book Trade by Vanwell Publishing Ltd., 1 Northrup Crescent, St. Catharines, Ontario L2M 6P5 ; in ENGLAND by T.F.H. Publications, PO Box 15, Waterlooville PO7 6BQ; in AUSTRALIA AND THE SOUTH PACIFIC by T.F.H. (Australia), Pty. Ltd., Box 149, Brookvale 2100 N.S.W., Australia; in NEW ZEALAND by Brooklands Aquarium Ltd. 5 McGiven Drive, New Plymouth, RD1 New Zealand; in Japan by T.F.H. Publications, Japan— Jiro Tsuda, 10-12-3 Ohjidai, Sakura, Chiba 285, Japan; in SOUTH AFRICA by Lopis (Pty) Ltd., P.O. Box 39127, Booysens, 2016, Johannesburg, South Africa. Published by T.F.H. Publications, Inc.
MANUFACTURED IN THE
UNITED STATES OF AMERICA
BY T.F.H. PUBLICATIONS, INC.

A NEW OWNER'S GUIDE TO
LABRADOR RETRIEVERS

MARY FEAZELL

Contents

The Labrador is a very athletic breed.

Labradors are trained to retrieve at a
very early age.

Your Labrador's health will show in his
overall appearance.

Nylabones® are safe chewing pacifiers for your Labrador.

The Labrador has a short, straight and dense coat that requires little grooming.

DESIGNER GENES the History and Origin

**F**eeling rather mischievous one day, Mother Nature decided to combine a pig for intelligence and wallowing, an African termite for wood appetite and earth-moving abilities, and finally added an otter for love of fun and water—out came a Labrador puppy!

The true origin of the Labrador Retriever has yet to be found, though many theories have been proposed. The long-sought mother country of Labrador Retrievers may possibly be Portugal. A most respected breeder/author, Mary Roslin-Williams, in her treasured 1969 book, *The Dual Purpose Labrador,* very briefly reported discovering in an Italian museum a

The right gene combination has given our present-day Labrador a most playful personality.

picture of a dark yellow Portuguese dog greatly resembling a Labrador Retriever. Following this random thread leads to an ancient breed, Cão de Castro Laboreiro, from the northern tip of Portugal. Its place of origin is Castro Laboreiro, "village of laborers," from which the dog received its name.

The striking similarities in the Laboreiro description and the modern Labrador Retriever are:

Height—20 to 25 inches.

Labradors take to water with great enthusiasm. This Labrador is heading out on a retrieve.

Weight—44 to 88 pounds.
Coat—medium short, harsh, waterproof.
Color—black, gray-black, gray, brindle, masked fawn.

General Appearance—muscles are densely packed, giving him a well-built overall appearance. He is exceedingly quick and mobile. The breed is bright and learns quickly but uses its own judgment in decisions.

Some differences are: the Laboreiro is used as a cattle guard, is suspicious of strangers and has an unusual vocal range. This Portuguese dog could answer some of the questions about solid coat colors, mismarks, conformation and gene strength in the Labrador Retriever. However, the differences provoke more questions as to how today's breed became the premier

Labrador Retrievers love all people, especially their owners.

retriever in the world and why the temperament changed from a suspecting guard to having such a promiscuous love of humans (our current Lab may hold a flashlight for a burglar). In 1501, Portugal was among the few nations to send fishing fleets to the east coast of Canada. Is the word Labrador an anglicized conjunction of the Portuguese words Llavador (farmer) and Laboreiro (laborer)? Perhaps someday a wandering researcher will weave the global black, yellow and chocolate threads into a complete historical tapestry.

Until then, we will rely on what serious breed biographers have documented. That is, the country of discovery of Labrador Retrievers is Canada, specifically St. John's Island off the coast of Newfoundland. It is known that the habitat didn't support native wild dogs.

The sailors and settlers, who brought dogs with them, did not live by fish alone and hunted any available game. The Labrador's "fish fetching" habits were so unique that this characteristic has been emphasized in the history books. Labradors were used to retrieve anything edible, as well as equipment, from land or water and for draft, all in the aid of both human and canine survival in the terribly hostile environment.

THE LABRADOR IN ENGLAND

Further breed development occurred when Canadian exports were brought by sailors into England, drawing the fancy of such noblemen as the Earls of Malmesbury and the Dukes of Buccleuch in the early 1800s. Three of the most often quoted early descriptions came from English sportsmen. Colonel Peter Hawker in 1830 described the Labrador Retriever as "by far the best for any kind of shooting. He

First and foremost, the Labrador Retriever is a hunting dog. He is an essential part of any hunter's gear.

is generally black and scarcely bigger than a Pointer, very fine in legs, with short, smooth hair and does not carry his tail so much curled as the other; is extremely quick, running, swimming and fighting ...and their sense of smell is hardly to be credited...." The Third Earl of Malmesbury (1807-1889) wrote, "...the real breed may be known by their having a close coat which turns water off like oil, and, above all, a tail like an otter." In 1873 Stonehenge included in his description of the breed that "The evidences of good temper must be regarded with great care since his utility depends on his disposition." In 40 years the breed had changed from being described as "quick in fighting" to "good temper." Other references of the time used terms such as docile and obedient.

In the early years of importation, Labradors remained in the hands of English nobility and upper class sportsmen who had no economic interests in breeding, needing only to continue a useful retriever for their hunts. The dogs were referred to only as "retrievers" since they neither pointed nor flushed as did other breeds. The Third Earl of Malmesbury is credited with permanently adding the name Labrador in his 1887 letter to the Sixth Duke of Buccleuch "We always call mine Labrador dogs..."

The genetic strength of the Labrador was proven when it was

The Labrador is an excellent retriever both on land and in water.

Labradors are strongly built dogs and natural athletes. bred to many other breeds in England; the resulting puppies looked like Labradors, picking up only minor characteristics from the outcrosses. The hound and mastiff influences can still be slightly noticed in some of today's less typical Labrador specimens. On January 3, 1905, the process for separate registration for the breed with The (English) Kennel Club was completed. Lord Knutsford wrote a Standard (detailed description) for Labradors in 1923 that has changed very little, only slightly expanded in their current Standard. The (English) Labrador Retriever Club was formed in 1916.

THE LABRADOR IN THE UNITED STATES

On the boat again—back to North America. In 1917 the American Kennel Club registered the first Labrador Retriever, Brocklehirst Floss (AKC # 223339), a bitch from Scotland. The eastern flyway with its abundant game called for an excellent retriever. It became fashionable among the wealthy New Yorkers to have pheasant shoots and duck hunts. Soon they were importing more Labradors and Scottish trainers and gamekeepers. Some of the well known families who helped establish the breed in the United States were: Harriman, Gould, Belmont, du Pont, Morgan, Brokaw, Lord, Field.

A national (parent) club, as recognized by the American Kennel Club, does not use a geographical description in its name other than America, if they so wish. The Labrador Retriever Club, Inc. did not choose that option. A local area club for a breed must be granted permission for establishment from the national club, must choose a name representative of their immediate locale and must work through the difficult AKC process before becoming licensed to hold conformation shows, obedience trials and hunt tests at which are awarded AKC title points. No area breed club may hold licensed field trials for retrievers. These trials are held either by the national club or specific retriever clubs created only for field trial purposes.

Firsts for the Breed
• The American Kennel Club granted full and separate **recognition** to Labrador Retrievers on February 1, 1932.

Controlled chaos—1988 National Specialty Show Open Black Class, Arlington, Texas.

The Labrador Retriever has claimed far more field trial championships than all other breeds combined.

• **The Labrador Retriever Club, Inc. (LRC)** was incorporated in the State of New York on October 7, 1931 with Mrs. Marshall Field serving as founding president with vice-presidents Robert Goelet and Franklin Lord, and secretary-treasurer Wilton Lloyd-Smith completing the slate.

• Mr. Lord chose Monday, December 21, 1931, as the date to run the Club's first **field trial**, as he wished to keep it private with no gallery. The trial took place on 8000 acres of Glenmere Court Estate owned by Mr. Robert Goelet near Chester, New York. Judges David Wagstaff of Tuxedo Park, NY, and Dr. Samuel Milbank of New York, NY, had an entry of 16 in the Open Stake and 11 in the American Bred Stake. A yellow dog, Carl of Boghurst, owned by Mrs. Marshall Field was the winner of the Open Stake and Sam of Arden, Mr. Harriman's black dog, was the winner of the American Bred Stake.

• On Thursday, May 18, 1933, the first **National Specialty show** was held in the garage of Marshall Field's townhouse on 76th Street in New York City. This show offered three classes: Puppy, Novice, and Limit, with dogs and bitches being shown together in each class. Thirty-three Labradors were entered for Mrs. Field to judge. The Best of Breed winner was Franklin Lord's Boli of Blake.

The Labrador's popularity continues to grow. Its good looks, loyalty and devotion to its owner are just some of the reasons why.

• The earliest **local area breed club** for Labrador Retrievers is the LRC of Hawaii, established in 1971.

• The Labrador Retriever Club hosted its own National Specialty show only on the East Coast for 43 years. Helen Ginnel (Whygin), a director of LRC, strongly encouraged the Club to **rotate its national show** throughout the U.S. In 1976, three Pacific coast area Labrador clubs joined forces to host the national show. In the ensuing years "the National" has rotated through the time zones, being hosted by many area clubs. In 1996 the National Specialty again became separate, with LRC hosting its own show near Boston,

Dog shows provide wonderful opportunities to meet other people who love Labrador Retrievers and to learn to work closely with your dog.

complete with Hunting Retriever Tests.

There are now 21 licensed area Labrador Retriever clubs and more at the sanctioned level located across the whole of the United States. The American Kennel Club at 51 Madison Avenue, New York, NY 10010 has the name and address of the contact person, usually the secretary, for The Labrador Retriever Club, Inc. Packets of breed and area club information are available.

First Champions of the Breed

Bench (Show) Champion Ch. Boli of Blake. Whelped 1932 (Eng. Ch. Ingleston Ben x Banchory Trace). Breeder: Lady Howe. Owner: Franklin Lord.

Field Trial Champion FC Blind of Arden. Whelped 1933 (Odds On x Peggy of Shipton). Breeder/owner: Hon. W. Averill Harriman.

Dual Champion Dual Ch. Michael of Glenmere. Whelped 1935 (Ace of Whitmore x Vixen of Glenmere). Breeder: R. Goelet. Owner: J. Angle.

Amateur Field Trial Champion (est. 9/14/1951) AFC Jupiter of Avandale. Whelped 10/08/46 (L'ile Larry x Keith's Bonnie Teal). Owner: F. R. Bacon, Jr.

National Field Champion (est. 1942) '42 NFC Dual Ch. Shed of Arden. Whelped 1939 (Ch. Raffles of Earlsmoor x FC Decoy of Arden). Breeder: W.A. Harriman. Owner: Paul Bakewell III.

National Amateur Field Champion (est. 1957) '58 NAFC Dual Ch. Boley's Tar Baby (King Chukker of Robinsdale x Mem of Greeymar). Owner: Bing Grunwald.

Utility Dog Tracking Uneva Trouper UDT. Breeder/owner: Josephine Mills.

Obedience Trial Champion (est. 7/1/1977) OTCH Royal Oaks Tar of Dorcliffe TD. Whelped 2/11/1968 ('67 NFC, AFC Buttes Blue Moon x Ch Shamrock Acres Whygin Tardy CD). Breeder: Mrs. Charles Allen. Owner: Buzz Taylor. Title: 4/9/1978.

Master Hunter (est. 2/9/1985) Oakwicks's

Thundering Jake MH (FC, AFC Sunday's Texas Thunderburr x Varner Creek Happy Teal). Owner: James R. Vaughan.

This most recent sporting event, created primarily for hunters and offering Junior and Senior levels as well as Master, is judged only on a "pass-fail" basis rather than on competitive placement. The Hunting Retriever Tests (HRTs) have been one of the American Kennel Club's greatest successes.

Retriever Achievers

Spanning the nearly 80 years and the millions of Labradors in America, it is still a rare dog or bitch who has truly founded a dynasty that stands and continues to produce excellent dogs for decades. Some of the most important producers who may still be found in or behind current pedigrees are:

1995 Westminster Kennel Club Best of Breed winner Ch. Graemoor Tim owned by Kendall Herr and Betty Graham.

'42 NFC Dual Ch. Shed of Arden (whelped 1937). Owner, W. A. Harriman.

Sire: Ch. Raffles of Earlmoor.

Dam: FC Decoy of Arden (first bitch field champion).
Ch. Shamrock Acres Light Brigade (whelped 7/6/
64). Owners, Sally McCarthy and Mrs. James Getz.
Sire: Ch. Shamrock Acres Casey Jones CD.
Dam: Ch. Whygin Busy Belinda.
Ch. Lockerbie Brian Boru (whelped 9/1/67).
Owner, Marjorie Brainard.
Sire: Ch. Lockerbie Kismet.
Dam: Lockerbie Tackety Boots.
'68 NFC, '67 & '68 NAFC Super Chief (whelped 6/
27/62). Owner, August Belmont.
Sire: FC, AFC Paha Sapa Chief II.
Dam: Ironwoods Cherokee Chica.
NFC, AFC San Joaquin Honcho (whelped 1/23/73).
Owner, Judy Weikel Aycock.
Sire: FC, AFC Trumarc's Raider.
Dam: Doxie Gypsy Taurus.
Wyntercreek Autumn Tyee WC.
Breeder, Mary Jane Sarbaugh.
Sire: Can. Ch. Ballyduff Johnson.
Dam: Somersett Snowstorm WC.
Big River Mancy (Bitch, whelped 5/18/69). Owner,
Harry Sinz.
Sire: FC, AFC My Rebel.
Dam: Big River Daphne.
Ch. Lockerbie Shillelagh (Bitch). Owners, Ceylon
and Marjorie Brainard.

Ch. Wyndcall's Rampant and Wyndcall Heatherhill Spark bred by Nancy Stewart and Mary Feazell.

Sire: Ch. Lockerbie Sandylands Tarquin.
Dam: Princess of Marlow.
Ballyduff Lark (Bitch, whelped. 6/25/78). Owners, Chris Kofron & Mary Wiest.
Sire: Eng. Ch. Timspring Sirius.
Dam: Spark of Ballyduff.
Cobbs Yellow Frenzy CDX, WC (Bitch). Owners, Cheryl and Lon Ostenson.
Sire: Lucky Four Finnigan O'Riagain.
Dam: Chamber's California Chablis.

The Labrador Retriever should be a medium sized, well balanced retriever gundog.

Ch. Shamrock Acres Light Brigade.

CHARACTERISTICS of the Labrador

Since the beginning the Labrador Retriever has been, is now and, hopefully, will always be first and foremost a working gun dog. The breed's strengths, soundness and temperament all depend on breeders maintaining the retrieving ability. The second most important characteristic is the Labrador's great and constant need for human companionship. A unique and consistent trait is the breed's ability to love and bond at any age, unlike many other breeds. It takes a ten-year-old adult the same length of time to love a new master as it does an eight-week-old puppy. These three attributes influence every Labrador Retriever's action or reaction.

Utility was an important factor in the original purpose of the Labrador. For this reason, the dog had to be a strong swimmer.

Since 1991, Labrador Retrievers have been the most popular breed in the U.S. of all the breeds the American Kennel Club recognizes, with well over 100,000 registered each year. Besides being great hunting dogs and family members, they are increasingly useful as guide dogs, physical-service dogs, hearing dogs and therapy dogs. Labs are used in search and rescue, cadaver searches, manhunts and evidence searches. In detection, Labradors are highly effective in arson, toxic waste, gas leaks and narcotics, where they must work in dangerous, difficult situations with different handlers than those who trained them. The quick bonding ability of Labradors is particularly important in these circumstances. The depths of the breed's abilities have yet to be explored. However, with their overwhelming instinct to retrieve, Labs can make bomb squads a little twitchy.

All relationships, including dog-human, are two-way

affairs. Many books only discuss what the "right" breed may be for the interested person; however, we must also see the world and the people inhabiting it from a *Labrador's point of view (LV)*.

LABRADOR'S HOMES AND GARDENS

The best owner for a Lab? Hunters, of course...not necessarily. Only if they are willing to make house dogs of the Labradors, which is contrary to how most bird dog breeds are kenneled. *LV: I did a great job finding all your birds today, then you leave me outside; perhaps I should sing.* Labradors do not take much grooming, but must have as much people-time as it is possible for their families to give in order to reach their full potential. Lying on the kitchen floor waiting for a crumb to drop constitutes quality time to a Lab as does sleeping next to a child's bed.

If a household member has allergies that would preclude having a dog in the house, consider a breed that does well as an outside dog only—it should **not** be a Labrador.

The family wants a watchdog. Investigate breeds that are bred for that job. Labradors are not. In fact, reputable breeders will not breed the rare atypical

The Labrador is generally patient and accepting of other animals. Moon and Juanita are getting to know each other. Owner, Connie Howard.

aggressive individual. Labradors are gentle friends to the world.

As a watchdog, the Labrador Retriever will fail. He will welcome any burglar with a wagging tail.

"We own acreage/farm/ ranch and want the dog to run loose." The Labrador will usually last two weeks; it is often the owner who runs over him. Labradors have no fear of moving or still vehicles and will sleep under the car, jump out of a pickup truck at 70 miles an hour or nonchalantly stroll in front of a hurtling 18-wheeled truck. Fencing is simply mandatory. The Labrador is a hunting dog with an uncanny sense of smell. *LV: Wow! there are birds and a lady wearing perfume just over there.* Over there may well be a mile or three away across the Interstate.

If the family interests lie in gardening and horticulture, Labs can provide interesting, unique effects as they are indeed in the excavating and re-scaping business. *LV: There can never be enough holes.* There will always be one hole big enough for the Lab to keep its entire body cool. The owner usually finds it after dark.

For owners who do not have time to train a dog, an older well-trained Labrador would be a better option.

Are you and the Labrador Retriever right for each other? If it is to be a trained house dog and well-fenced-in when unsupervised, yes. Under these conditions, by five years of age, Labs can become almost human. *LV: Can we negotiate about the couch?* Ninety-five percent of what the owner receives from the Labrador is a direct result of what the owner has put into him or her; five percent depends on the individual dog.

Ideally, the wisest prospective owners will complete a few very important, self-protective assignments prior to speaking to a breeder. Read as many books on the Labrador Retriever as possible, preparing a list of questions. There is no such thing as a dumb question.

Call a veterinarian's office asking for a local Labrador breed club or an all-breed kennel club's telephone number; they are not normally listed in the telephone directory. The Labrador area club will have referrals for breeders, specifics about the Labrador Rescue Program and listings of obedience and field training clubs. If the information is unavailable in the local area, call the American Kennel Club in New York City, NY or Raleigh, NC for the national Labrador Retriever Club's current contact person's name and address.

Visit some obedience classes and make inquiries as to cost, if there is a waiting list and how many weeks the sessions last. The family needs to discuss the responsibilities of daily training, as well as care, and who is to take the Labrador puppy or adult to classes each week. As even the smartest children are not born

Marsh Dak's Shooting Star, CD, a black Labrador Retriever in an advanced obedience class. Owner, Dianne L. Schlemmer.

knowing table manners or ABCs, neither is the most intelligent Labrador. A Labrador is not just a fashionable, temporary possession, but a lifelong family member.

What Am I To You

*As a pup I dreamed and wondered
What life would hold in store
For ME, I thought, there's something great
Beyond that kennel door.*

Labrador Retriever puppies learn a lot from their littermates, such as how to play, compete and find lost food.

Your Labrador Retriever will benefit from obedience lessons, and once he has learned the basics you can go on to teach him tricks.

*Out there are needy people
And I have much to give
Love and wit and gentleness
To help them live*

I'd be someone's protector
Keep little ones from harm
Or guide an old man's weary footsteps
Or help to run a farm.

I'd run and bark and jump and play
With friends along a sandy shore
I'd roll in meadows thick and green
That lie beyond that kennel door.

Labradors enjoy
pleasing their
owners. They wish
nothing more than
spending their day
with the one who
trains them.

I lay here waiting...longing
As the days and years went by
My owner kept me fed and brushed
But, inside let me die.

26

I do not think of greatness now
I'm old and filled with pain.
My owner has some ribbons
But I have lived in vain.

I cannot think what could have been
My dreams are filled with hope no more.
Just floor and walls and broken heart
For me beyond this kennel door.

M. Kimmer

Before you purchase your puppy, it is a good idea to see the entire litter. Littermates often snuggle up together for warmth.

METHODS AND MYTHS

When choosing the breed that is number one in popularity, a great deal of caution must be exercised. Far too many owners think all one must do is own a Labrador in order to breed one. Avoid at all costs those sellers who cannot or will not answer your questions. A knowledgeable breeder will provide recommendations for veterinary care, reading lists, names of reputable boarding facilities and trustworthy field trainers. As difficult as it is emotionally, this long term decision should not be rushed. Adult or puppy, in Labradors there is a choice. If toddlers or elderly persons are part of the home, if time constraints prohibit obedience training or the household decor cannot withstand a puppy, seriously consider a well-trained adult Labrador. The savings in veterinary bills, hours of obedience training, wear and tear on both the house and your patience are enormous. As Labradors live anywhere from 11 to 15 years, lasting longer than the family's next three cars, age is not of great concern.

When the time comes, it is important that you visit both the adult relatives and the environment in which the

puppies were raised. A caring breeder will be available and interested in helping with health questions, training problems and sharing the laughter from the inevitable funny happenings for the rest of the dog's life. This breeder's care is part of what is received in the price of the Labrador. As breeders have no wish to be interfering grandparents, the buyer is always encouraged to keep in touch with the breeder.

FAIRY TALES

Females Are Sweeter/Smarter than Males

Neither sex nor color have anything to do with a Labrador's individual personality, nature and nurture form the temperament. In many Labrador lines (families), the males are more loving and less independent than the females.

Although Labradors love to be outside, they do not thrive as solely outdoor dogs—they belong inside with the family.

One Color Is Preferable Over Another

Color has an impact only on the human eye. What is far more important than color, sex or age are temperament, good health and longevity. These are the qualities that impact both the owner's daily life with the Labrador and the family's contribution to the veterinarian's annual income. Color decision should be based on whether the owner minds the hair showing in the butter or on the carpet.

As proud and strong as the Labrador Retriever may be, he is not a guard dog. Pay no attention to myths leading you to believe this to be true.

Large Black Labradors Make Good Guard Dogs

No Labrador is designed to be a guard dog. The pain that must be inflicted on a gentle, loving Labrador to make it aggressive can force the dog into psychosis. These afflicted individuals sadly must be destroyed as they become untrustworthy with anyone, including their owners.

Puppies Must Go to Their New Homes on the 49th Day

Two very important words have been lost in this statement. For Labradors it should read: "Puppies must NOT go to their new homes BEFORE the 49th day." The 49th day theory was formulated in the 1930s by people experimenting with a herding/guard dog breed. This idea is the exact opposite of what is true in Labradors, which are one of the few unique breeds that love and bond at any age. As the result of this marvelous quality, prospective owners are free to consider any age Labrador whether from a breeder or a rescue program.

Pet-Quality Is Cheaper

In any litter, each puppy, whatever its quality, costs the breeder the exact same amount of money and loving labor to be brought into the world and raised. Most litters produce few show-quality puppies. These future stars are very difficult to recognize by eight weeks. A show-quality puppy is normally reserved for the breeder or sold only to another breeder/exhibitor. However, upon seeing adult pets of their own breeding, breeders have often been heard to moan "Oh, I sold the wrong puppy again."

Rare Colors or White Labrador Advertisements

Two "don'ts": don't be a fool and don't bother!

Labradors come in three colors: black, chocolate and yellow. Rare colors would indicate the puppies may not be purebred even if they have papers. At best these are mismarks and cannot be registered. Breeders who advertise "white" are publicly proving their own ignorance. A yellow is a yellow, and is never referred to as white, buff, blonde or golden. A Golden Retriever is an entirely separate long-coated breed. Yellow Labrador puppies' coats usually darken as they shed through all their different puppy coats. They may start life as a very "light cream," but there is no guarantee that it will be the same color as the adult coat. Although all colors of Labrador puppies are born with dark blue eyes, the color changes to brown very quickly. A blue- or green-eyed older puppy or adult Labrador proves without any doubt that there is a "fence jumper" in the pedigree. Lighter brown eyes bordering on gold or yellow occur occasionally in purebred Labradors. Sometimes, but not always, the lighter eyes indicate a chocolate gene. These light "bird of prey" eyes are not preferred.

An expert breeder will strive for excellence in each and every litter raised.

Types of Breeders

Hobby

The hobby breeder's primary goal is excellence, not dollars. Generational improvement is sought in every breeding. This person will remove from a breeding program any Labrador who has or produces a serious genetic fault regardless of titles or how much time and money have been invested in that Labrador. They will be "students of the breed," continually searching out new information on genetics, diseases, training or other related aspects. They may have kennels or their dogs may all be house dogs.

Professional

Some professionals also strive for excellence in breeding, particularly if additional income is derived from boarding and or training dogs. They will have kennels. Ask if they compete in any AKC events.

Casual

Often referred to as "back yard" breeders. These people are not students of the breed nor are they interested in gaining any knowledge.

One-Time Breeder

"We just wanted her to have one litter before she is spayed because ..."

Rescue personnel unequivocally state, "If the one time only breeders would just not do that breeding, there would be almost no Labradors in the pounds, shelters or rescue programs."

A young hunting dog gets his first taste of waterfowl, although he seems more interested in tasting his puppy food.

Fin and Feather Breeders

A breeder with a hunting or field performance background has quite likely done some specialized socialization. From the first pan feeding of dog food, the breeder may have called "come, come, come" all the way from kitchen to whelping box. This action associates the "recall" with any Labrador's favorite event—food. When puppies are responding happily to being called, loud noises are added from far away to the "come" command, usually the banging of kitchen pot lids or the firing of a cap pistol in another room. At first, the puppies are appropriately frightened as the flight response is necessary for survival in the wild. If the noise and command are consistently given with each and every feeding (and the neighbors do not officially request the breeder's commitment to the funny farm), within approximately three days the fear has

Labrador Retriever puppies intended for field work are sometimes trained with a boat bumper or fender with a rope tied to the end of it. been eliminated and association of loud noises with food has been imprinted. Do NOT, however, presume that a 12-gauge shotgun may now be fired close to a puppy without making it gun shy. Labradors may be water dogs, but water and swimming must still be introduced correctly. Throwing puppies or adults in the water does not come under the definition of correctly and can create incurable, life long problems. When the puppies are four weeks old, putting a low-sided large pan of water in the puppy pen will start the introduction. The first swim should be a pleasant experience. If the day is hot enough to make the puppies pant slightly, cool, not cold, water will feel wonderful. Any container, from a swimming pool to a child' s wading pool, as long as it is deep enough to be swimming water for the puppies, will work. Each puppy should be held and eased into the

Labradors love splashing around in the water, especially with friends. water; hands are not completely removed until the puppy is swimming. Weather permitting, swimming practice can be a daily event until the puppies go to their new homes. *LV: Water feels so good it should be shared. Shake as close as possible to humans.*

"Wing testing" is the observation of puppies' responses to feathers. A game bird wing is dropped into the whelping box or puppy pen. Notes are taken as to which puppy is interested or not, smells, carries, takes the wing from another puppy, runs away with the prize or approaches the human observer with it. Later, individual puppies are tested alone and away from littermates, but in a location familiar to the puppy. Tying (no hooks) the bird wing to a fishing pole with monofilament line gives yet another perspective and for the puppy eliminates the distraction of human movement.

CERTIFICATION OF HIPS AND EYES

"OFA is a field title."

When the experienced Labrador caller could not stop laughing, the "casual breeder" hung up on her.

Good breeders of Labradors have had their breeding stock x-rayed and certified clear of dysplasia (malformation of hip and elbow joints) by the Orthopedic Foundation for Animals (OFA). They also have had a current (within the last 12 months) eye examination done by an American College of Veterinary Ophthalmology (ACVO) diplomat prior to breeding. The Canine Eye Registration Foundation (CERF) is

As Labrador puppies mature, it is wise to have a veterinarian who will give a temporary consultation regarding hips. Certification from a screening agency is received after the age of two years.

an organization specializing in registering dogs whose eyes have been thoroughly tested for problems. A veterinarian in general practice cannot certify eyes, any more than humans can get glasses from their family doctor. Labradors can only receive permanent OFA certification after two years of age; however, OFA will give a temporary consultation opinion before two years. ACVO eye examinations are good for one year as Labrador inherited eye diseases appear at different ages. As Labradors are very slow to mature, breeding before age two is not recommended. There is **no** excuse for breeding Labradors prior to being x-rayed and having an eye exam.

AMERICAN KENNEL CLUB

A buyer needs to know that the American Kennel Club (AKC) works on the honor system—all the more reason to buy from a reputable breeder. AKC registration does not imply or guarantee quality, but only shows that the puppies are eligible for registration in the stud book. AKC offers two types of registration: regular and limited. Both may be used in the same litter. A limited registration means the puppy is fully registered with AKC, but cannot be bred as an adult because its offspring cannot be registered. Limited registration does not imply there is anything wrong with the breeding or the puppy. It is the most wonderful tool AKC has given to breeders to help control the overpopulation of "disposable" Labradors flooding the rescue programs, pounds and shelters. Presently, most knowledgeable, caring breeders sell all pet puppies on limited registration. Limited

Limited registration allows breeders to control the overpopulation of Labradors—breeding should be left to experts.

Labrador Retriever clearing the bar jump at an agility trial. Agility trials allow all dogs to compete for titles.

registration may be changed only one time to regular and only by the breeder, but no breeder is ever under any obligation to do so. Limited or neutered Labradors may be entered in obedience trials and hunt tests but are not eligible for field trials or conformation shows.

SALES CONTRACT

The breeder may use a puppy sales contract. Extra copies are quite happily given to be taken home for review. A contract is recommended by many clubs as it is a clear reminder of all parties' responsibilities during the dog's life. The contractual agreement, AKC information, health records and feeding instructions may be combined in one document.

HEALTH RECORDS

"We haven't given any shots to the puppies because we wanted the owners to know for sure what shots were given and the owners would be much more confident in their own vets. That's why we're asking less money."

Luckily, the buyers were wearing running shoes that day.

When a puppy is received by the new owners, it should have had at least two of the first series of shots, plus two wormings. The accompanying complete health records should show the brand names, dosage amounts and dates given. Some breeders save the empty individual bottles of vaccine so the new owner may take them when the puppy makes its first visit to the veterinarian. As in any profession, there are good veterinarians and better ones. Ask the breeder's advice, choose carefully, then build as good a relationship with your veterinarian as is held with the family's doctor.

TERMINOLOGY

Common terms used by breeders, but not geneticists, are inbreeding, line-breeding, outcrossing and interbreds.

Inbreeding dramatically concentrates the genes as the same dogs are the repeated contributors to the gene pool. Most breeders will agree father-daughter, mother-son, full brother-sister all constitute inbreeding. This type of breeding should be done **only** with absolutely superior animals and only by a breeder who has bred, lived with and genetically tested at least the last four

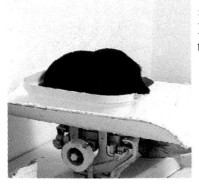

This Labrador puppy is being weighed at the veterinarian's office. Puppies should have at least one visit to the vet before you bring them home.

Healthy and sound Labradors are produced by breeders who are aware of each dog's ancestry and who breed for specific traits.

generations of ancestors as inbreeding magnifies previously hidden traits.

The definition of line-breeding is blurred. This type of breeding will vary from breeding grandfather-granddaughter to what is termed a "gentle line-breeding," meaning having no common Labradors in the first three generations but having the same individual dogs repeated again and again in the fourth and fifth generations. Consistency of appearance and in temperament within the litter is usually good.

Outcrossing is the breeding of two totally unrelated Labradors. There is quite often no consistency in appearance; traits will be hidden but still carried. Development is unpredictable. Some form of outcrossing is necessary periodically to bring in new bloodlines.

Interbred means "mongrelization," the breeding of two dogs of different breeds or several breeds.

TITLES

The AKC does not recognize any foreign titles. Because of restricted space on pedigrees, all AKC Labrador Retriever titles are abbreviated as follows:

Due to their inherent retrieving abilities, Labrador Retrievers are very easy to train.

Prefixes

Ch.–Conformation Show Champion
FC–Field Champion
AFC–Amateur Field Champion
NFC–National Field Champion
NAFC–National Amateur Field Champion
DUAL Ch. or **DC**–Conformation and Field Champion. (AFC does not apply.)
OTCh.–Obedience Trial Champion
TRIPLE Ch. or **TC**–Dual and Obedience Trial Champion

Affixes

UDX–Utility Dog Excellent
UD–Utility Dog
CDX–Companion Dog Excellent

CD–Companion Dog
VST–Variable Surface Tracking
TDX–Tracking Dog Excellent
TD–Tracking Dog
TC–Tracking Champion (requires TD, TDX, & VST)

This is Ch. Finchingfield Freedom II being exhibited at an outdoor dog show.

MH—Master Hunter
SH—Senior Hunter
JH—Junior Hunter
CGC—Canine Good Citizen
WC—Working Certificate (Recognized by LRC, Inc., but not AKC.)

PEDIGREES

The puppy's pedigree should be on one sheet of paper. Beware of two kinds of pedigrees: multiple sheets with grandparents scattered all over and the extended with six or more generations.

Multiple pages frankly means the breeder was too uninformed to be able to correctly type a pedigree for the breeding or too parsimonious to pay for an AKC certified pedigree.

Seven-week-old puppies bred by Joe and Kim Petkosh. The blue and pink ribbons denote the sex of each puppy.

Extended pedigrees are usually used only to display the one or the very few champions far back in the puppy's ancestral history. These pedigrees are often connected with the term "championship lines" in

newspaper advertisements. The farther back in the pedigree, the less genetic influence the titled dog has on this breeding.

A dog pedigree is easier to read than many genealogical family trees. The sire's (father) family is always at the top. The dam's (mother) family takes the bottom half. Centered at the left, between the sire and dam, is the recorded Labrador. Percentage of genetic influence is included in the sample.

Three-Generation Pedigree

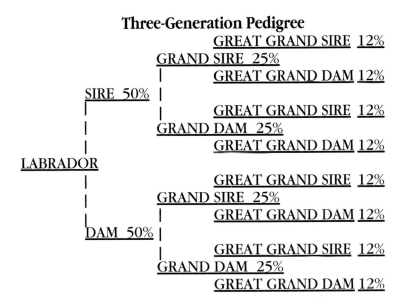

How To Speak Dog Fluently

A Labrador is "finished" when it completes its championship, not "championed out."

The abbreviation of champion, Ch., is always capitalized.

The past tense of spay is spayed, not spaydead.

A male is "standing at stud," not being "studded out."

A dog is registered, not "papered."

The true test of fluency is using the word "bitch" smoothly without stammering for 30 seconds before or blushing longer afterwards.

SELECTING Your Labrador Puppy

It is important to know if a particular litter is within the family budget, but the initial telephone call will receive a much more lengthy response from the breeder if the caller is a little less direct. Name introductions and a description of the desired puppy are given first. If the particular puppy is available, then the cost is asked; if not, the cost is irrelevant. Prices are not negotiable, though often payment plans may be discussed. In a payment plan, a bill of sale must be given, but AKC papers are held by the breeder until the final amount is paid. Though Labrador adults adjust very well to changes at any age, young puppies should not go to their new homes prior to their seventh week, eight weeks is even better. The mental growth that occurs in the socialization patterns with the dam and littermates during these weeks cannot be recaptured at any other time in the Labrador's life. "Buyer beware" of breeders who allow puppies to leave the litter at six weeks or before.

Selecting your new Labrador Retriever puppy is not always easy. Most pups seem to have adoring eyes that long to have you take them home.

Expect Richter Scale reaction to inquiries for puppy purchases as either a surprise present or Christmas gift. Reputable breeders care too much about their puppies to sell to someone they have not met and the surprised owner undoubtedly would not have chosen the same puppy. If purchasing a puppy near Christmas, make plans to take it home well after the day of bedlam, there is just too much excitement and too many dangerous items available. In this manner Christmas will be extended and the puppy will be the center of attention, making its adjustment far easier and much more safe.

FIRST VISIT

Limit your time to an hour or less. A breeder's family is

as busy as anyone's would be if one of the adults held two full-time jobs. If done correctly, being a breeder/exhibitor is a full-time job, but does not pay, so another occupation is quite often necessary. If an appointment has been made to visit a breeder, be on time. If you will be late, call to explain as would be done with any friend or client. Buyers have been removed from puppy waiting lists because the breeder became convinced they were not responsible enough to care for a Labrador properly. Before playing with puppies, ask to see the AKC blue individual registration forms for the puppies, the two (one for the sire and one for the dam) OFA certificates and two ACVO or CERF certificates, checking the dates of the eye examinations. It is just as easy to fall in love with a puppy from sound parents and a great deal less costly later. Having both parents certified does not absolutely guarantee the puppy will not develop problems as polygenetics as well as future growth environment play parts; however, parental clearances greatly reduce the odds. The adult dogs, with particular emphasis on the dam (mother), should be seen next. All puppies, piglets and porcupine babies are cute. If you do not care for the looks or behavior of the adults, then do not buy a puppy who will in just a few weeks look and act as these adults do. In all fairness to the dam of the litter, Mother Nature played another trick. Just when the breeder would like the dam to look her best for the prospective buyers, she is

Your Labrador puppy should be well socialized prior to your taking it home.

not wearing her best dress and indeed looks her very worst due to hormonal changes, pregnancy and caring for her babies. The sire may or may not be on the premises. The careful breeder's goal is generational improvement—to have each succeeding generation of puppies be better than the parents. To accomplish this frustrating feat the owner must know not only the faults and virtues of the bitch, but also her ancestors. Often the stud dog who

By looking at several good examples of the breed you will be able to know exactly what you are looking for in your new Labrador Retriever.

The original meaning of "puppy eyes." This is Driftwood Lucy at eight weeks, bred by Rob and Beverly Montgomery.

has the genetic ability to offset the faults and strengthen the virtues lives elsewhere, perhaps a thousand or more miles away. A picture of this grand specimen should be available. Copies of his orthopedic and eye clearances must also be available.

Ask the house rules before visiting with the puppies. It is not at all unusual for the breeder to request that shoes be left at the front door, the buyer wear clean clothes, wash his hands, or very young puppies not be handled. Sounds a bit fanatical?—not since the advent of parvo in 1978. Parvo is a killer; an airborne virus that rides on the bottom of shoes, on hair, hands and clothing. Visitors can be the carriers, particularly if they have traveled to more than one kennel in the same clothes. Consider this puppy visit in the same light as going to the neonatal section of a hospital. No matter how rigorous the house rules, those rules may be protecting YOUR puppy.

Check List Observations
Where were the puppies born?
Where are they now being kept?
Is there evidence of the breeder's long term involvement in the breed: pictures, awards, Labrador books and magazines?
Are all dog areas clean?
Do the puppies have toys?

Questions
Casual breeders may be separated from serious breeders by the answer to this one **most important question** the prospective purchaser should ask, "If at any

These nursing puppies are tagged with colored collars so the breeder can tell them apart and monitor their growth.

time in the future I cannot keep
the dog, would you be willing to
take it back regardless of age?"
An unequivocal yes is the
correct answer. The sales
contract may have a statement to
the effect that the breeder has
first option on return of the dog.

The buyer must understand that
the breeder may not be able to
purchase the dog back, but the
relief that the owner does not
have to give the Labrador to
*Carefully choosing a
Labrador Retriever will
ensure a happy, healthy
relationship between dog
and owner.*
strangers or make the drive to the dog pound is worth a
great deal more. How old are the sire and dam? How long
has the breeder been in Labradors? Is the breeder keeping
a puppy from this litter? (If the litter is not good enough
for the breeder, is it good enough for you?) How many
litters has the breeder bred? What did the breeder hope to
achieve in this litter? Will this be the bitch's only litter?
Also ask any other questions that developed when you
were researching the breed.

PURCHASING YOUR PUREBRED

When a family is comfortable with a breeder and likes
both the adult Labs and puppies, then it is time to ask
about their location on the puppy list, non-refundable
deposits to hold a puppy, and what type of AKC
registration will be used and the puppy's registered name.
Puppy lists are usually on a first come-first serve basis.
Non-refundable deposits protect all parties. They
guarantee the purchaser a puppy barring the death of the
puppy while still in the breeder's care, in which case the
deposit should be returned. The deposit also protects the
breeder from people who routinely try to hedge their bets
by putting their names on all available lists or those who
change their minds at the last second leaving the breeder
with additional advertising, feeding and veterinarian costs.

SPAYING AND NEUTERING

Discuss spaying and neutering with the breeder frankly. On very rare occasions the breeder may suggest that the puppy has a superior potential and should not be neutered until much later, if at all. Do not breed either dogs or bitches prior to neutering or spaying. They will not be exposed to venereal diseases nor can the permanent effects of hormonal changes during pregnancy occur in bitches. Neutered dogs cannot develop prostate or testicle cancer. Vasectomies are not usually recommended for dogs, as the effects of the surgery may actually create more problems later in life. Although the appearances are somewhat similar, dogs are very different from humans, including having a bone in the penis. Hysterectomies eliminate ovarian and uterine infections and cancer and help protect against mammary tumors.

MAKING THE CHOICE

Adult members should be aware of their family's energy level, making an attempt to choose a puppy accordingly. A "high rolling" puppy will drive a quiet family to distraction, whereas a calm puppy will soon bore the active family. Healthy Labradors as a whole are unlikely to be low energy youngsters. Plan to visit the litter more than once, as the best match for the buyer may be sleepy and unresponsive during the initial visit. Exercise, feeding and vaccinations greatly affect puppies at this age. Ask the breeder to bring out only the puppies that are available. The number from which to choose will depend upon the family's location on the waiting list.

Bigger is not better. The size of a puppy at birth or eight weeks is not necessarily indicative of the Labrador's size at full maturity in the fourth year. Unless something has occurred to frighten the whole litter, be cautious of the puppy who hides inside or behind any available shelter when approached by strangers. The puppy may just not feel well that day or the temperament may be less than ideal for a Labrador. Give serious consideration to an experienced, reputable breeder's recommendation. This breeder's main goal is to make a good match so the family will be satisfied and the puppy will be happy.

Be considerate. If lucky enough to have second or third pick from a litter, do not tell the breeder it is not convenient to make your choice when the proper time comes. There may be several more families waiting. If the delay is too long, the choice may be lost or the breeder may have to make the choice. Labrador puppies choose their new owners far more often than the owners select them. A puppy will crawl up a pants leg, give a special "nuzzle," or some other action that wiggles a nest in the heart of the buyer. If available, choose the puppy the family remembers and discusses most between visits.

No one would be able to choose among this litter of one-week-old pups. You will not be able to meet the litter for five or six more weeks.

STANDARD for the Labrador Retriever

A breed standard is a detailed description for each separate breed as written by the individual national (parent) club and approved by the American Kennel Club. In America, the first official Labrador Retriever Standard was approved October 7, 1931; the latest February 12, 1994, effective March 31, 1994. A dog must look like a Labrador and act as a retriever to be a Labrador Retriever. The Labrador Standard is not written just for show dogs. Every statement has a functional reason to protect the dog and affect the efficient retrieval of game. "Fancy dogs may be measured by any rule however artificial, but a shooting dog should be judged by points which are relevant to his work." (J.H. Walsh, 1887)

The Labrador should have a well-developed but not exaggerated forechest.

AKC STANDARD FOR THE LABRADOR RETRIEVER

General Appearance—The Labrador Retriever is a strongly built, medium-sized, short-coupled dog possessing a sound, athletic, well-balanced conformation that enables it to function as a retrieving gun dog; the substance and soundness to hunt waterfowl or upland game for long hours under difficult conditions; the character and quality to win in the show ring; and the temperament to be a family companion. Physical features and mental characteristics should denote a dog bred to perform as an efficient Retriever of game with a stable temperament suitable for a variety of pursuits beyond the hunting environment.

The most distinguishing characteristics of the Labrador Retriever are its short, dense, weather resistant coat; an "otter" tail; a clean-cut head with broad back skull and moderate stop; powerful jaws; and its "kind,"

friendly eyes, expressing character, intelligence and good temperament.

Above all, a Labrador Retriever must be well balanced, enabling it to move in the show ring or work in the field with little or no effort. The typical Labrador possesses style and quality without lumber or cloddiness. The Labrador is bred primarily as a working gun dog; structure and soundness are of great importance.

Size, Proportion and Substance—*Size***—**The height at the withers for a dog is 22 to 24 inches; for a bitch is 21 to 23 inches. Any variance greater than $^1/_2$ inch above or below these heights is a disqualification. Approximate weight of dogs and bitches in working condition: dogs 65 to 80 pounds; bitches 55 to 70 pounds.

The minimum height ranges set

The Labrador is bred primarily as a working gun dog; structure and soundness are of great importance.

forth in the paragraph above shall not apply to dogs or bitches under twelve months of age.

Proportion—Short coupled; length from the point of the shoulder to the point of the rump is equal to or slightly longer than the distance from the withers to the ground. Distance from the elbow to the ground should be equal to one half of the height at the withers. The brisket should extend to the elbows, but not perceptibly deeper. The body must be of sufficient length to permit a straight, free and efficient stride; but the dog should never appear low and long or tall and leggy in outline. *Substance*—Substance and bone proportionate to the overall dog. Light, "weedy" individuals are definitely incorrect; equally objectionable are cloddy lumbering specimens. Labrador Retrievers shall be shown in working condition well-muscled and without excess fat.

Am. Can. Bda. Ch. Wyndcall's Keep On Trucking, bred, owned and handled by the author.

Head—*Skull*—The skull should be wide; well developed but without exaggeration. The skull and foreface should be on parallel planes and of approximately equal length. There should be a moderate stop—the brow slightly pronounced so that the skull is not absolutely in a straight line with the nose. The brow ridges aid in defining the stop. The head should be clean-cut and free from fleshy cheeks; the bony structure of the skull chiseled beneath the eye with no prominence in the cheek. The skull may show some median line; the occipital bone is not conspicuous in mature dogs. Lips should not be squared off or pendulous, but fall away in a curve toward the throat. A wedge-shape head, or a head long and narrow in muzzle and back skull is incorrect as are massive, cheeky heads. The jaws are

powerful and free from snippiness—the muzzle neither long and narrow nor short and stubby. *Nose*—The nose should be wide and the nostrils well-developed. The nose should be black on black or yellow dogs, and brown on chocolates. Nose color fading to a lighter shade is not a fault. A thoroughly pink nose or one lacking in any pigment is a disqualification. *Teeth*—The teeth should be strong and regular with a scissors bite; the lower teeth just behind, but touching the inner side of the upper incisors. A level bite is acceptable, but not desirable. Undershot, overshot, or misaligned teeth are serious faults. Full dentition is preferred. Missing molars or pre-molars are serious faults. *Ears*—The ears should hang moderately close to the head, set rather far back, and somewhat low on the skull; slightly above eye level. Ears should not be large and heavy, but in proportion with the skull and reach to the inside of the eye when pulled forward. *Eyes*—Kind, friendly eyes imparting good temperament, intelligence and alertness are a hallmark of the breed. They should be of medium size, set well apart, and neither protruding nor deep set. Eye color should be brown in black and yellow Labradors, and brown or hazel in chocolates. Black, or yellow eyes give a harsh expression and are undesirable. Small eyes, set close together or round prominent eyes are not typical of the breed. Eye rims are black in black and yellow Labradors; and brown in chocolates. Eye rims without pigmentation is a disqualification.

The teeth of your Labrador should be strong and regular with a scissors bite.

Labrador eye color should be brown in black and yellow Labradors, and brown or hazel in chocolates.

Neck, Topline and Body—*Neck*—The neck should be of proper length to allow the dog to retrieve game easily. It should be muscular and free from throatiness. The neck should rise strongly from the shoulders with a moderate arch. A short, thick neck or a "ewe" neck is incorrect. *Topline*—The back is strong and the topline is level from the withers to the croup when standing or moving. However, the loin should show evidence of flexibility for athletic endeavor. *Body*—The Labrador should be short-coupled, with good spring of ribs tapering to a moderately wide chest. The Labrador should not be narrow chested; giving the appearance of hollowness between the front legs, nor should it have a wide spreading, bulldog-like front. Correct chest conformation will result in tapering between the front legs that allows unrestricted forelimb movement. Chest breadth that is either too wide or too narrow for efficient movement and stamina is incorrect. Slab-sided individuals are not typical of the breed; equally objectionable are rotund or barrel chested specimens. The underline is almost straight, with little or no tuck-up in mature animals. Loins should be short, wide and strong; extending to well developed, powerful hindquarters. When viewed from the side, the Labrador Retriever shows a well-developed, but not exaggerated forechest. *Tail*—The tail is a distinguishing feature of the breed. It should be very thick at the base, gradually tapering toward the tip, of medium length, and extending no longer than to the hock. The tail should be free from feathering and clothed thickly all around with the Labrador's short, dense coat, thus having that peculiar rounded appearance that has been described as the "otter" tail. The tail should follow the topline in repose or when in motion. It may be carried gaily, but should not curl over the back. Extremely short tails or long thin tails are serious faults. The tail completes the balance of the Labrador by giving it a flowing line from the top of the head to the tip of the tail. Docking or otherwise altering the length or natural carriage of the tail is a disqualification.

Forequarters—Forequarters should be muscular; well

coordinated and balanced with the hindquarters. *Shoulders*—The shoulders are well laid-back, long and sloping, forming an angle with the upper arm of approximately 90 degrees that permits the dog to move his forelegs in an easy manner with strong forward reach. Ideally, the length of the shoulder blade should equal the length of the upper arm. Straight shoulder blades, short upper arms or heavy muscled or loaded shoulders, all restricting free movement, are incorrect. *Front Legs*—When viewed from the front, the legs should be straight with good strong bone. Too much bone is as undesirable as too little bone, and short legged, heavy boned individuals are not typical of the breed. Viewed from the side, the elbows should be directly under the withers, and the front legs should be perpendicular to the ground and well under the body. The elbows should be close to the ribs without looseness. Tied-in elbows or being "out at the elbows" interfere with free movement and are serious faults. Pasterns should be strong and short and should slope slightly from the perpendicular line of the leg. Feet are strong and compact, with well-arched toes and well-developed pads. Dew claws may be removed. Splayed feet, hare feet, knuckling over, or feet turning in or out are serious faults.

The "otter" tail is a distinguishing feature of the breed. It should be thick at the base, gradually tapering towards the tip.

Hindquarters—The Labrador's hindquarters are broad, muscular and well-developed from the hip to the hock with well-turned stifles and strong short hocks. Viewed from the rear, the hind legs are straight and parallel. Viewed from the side, the angulation of the rear legs is in balance with the front. The hind legs are strongly boned, muscled with moderate angulation at the stifle, and powerful, clearly defined thighs. The stifle is strong and there is no slippage of the patellae while in motion or when standing. The hock joints are strong, well let down and do not slip or hyper-extend while in motion or when standing. Angulation of both stifle and hock joint is such as to achieve the optimal balance of drive and traction. When standing, the rear toes are only slightly behind the point of the rump. Over angulation

The Labrador Retriever coat colors are black, yellow and chocolate. This colorful trio is owned by Jim and Debbie Gardner.

produces a sloping topline not typical of the breed. Feet are strong and compact, with well-arched toes and well-developed pads. Cow-hocks, spread hocks, sickle hocks and over-angulation are serious structural defects and are to be faulted.

Coat—The coat is a distinctive feature of the Labrador Retriever. It should be short, straight and very dense giving a fairly hard feeling to the hand. The Labrador should have a soft, weather-resistant undercoat that provides protection from water, cold and all types of ground cover. A slight wave down the back is permissible. Woolly coats, soft silky coats, and sparse slick coats are not typical of the breed, and

The coat of the Labrador is short, straight and very dense. The undercoat is soft and weather-resistant.

should be severely penalized.

Color—The Labrador Retriever coat colors are black, yellow and chocolate. Any other color or a combination of colors is a disqualification. A small white spot on the chest is permissible, but not desirable. White hairs from aging or scarring are not to be misinterpreted as brindling. *Black*—Blacks are all black. A black with brindle markings or a black with tan markings is a disqualification. *Yellow*—Yellows may range in color from fox-red to light cream, with variations in shading on the ears, back and underparts of the dog. *Chocolate*—Chocolates can vary in shade from light to dark chocolate. Chocolate with brindle or tan markings is a disqualification.

Movement—Movement of the Labrador Retriever should be free and effortless. When watching a dog

61

Movement as well as structure are passed along from parent to offspring.

move toward oneself, there should be no sign of elbows out. Rather the elbows should be held neatly to the body with the legs not too close or weaving, the legs should form straight lines, with all parts moving in the same plane. Upon viewing the dog from the rear, one should have the impression that the hind legs move as nearly as possible in a parallel line with the front legs. The hocks should do their full share of the work, flexing well, giving the appearance of power and strength. When viewed from the side, the shoulders should move freely and effortlessly, and the foreleg should reach forward close to the ground with extension. A short, choppy movement or high knee action indicates a straight shoulder; paddling indicates long, weak pasterns; and a short, stilted rear gait indicates a straight rear assembly; all are serious faults. Movement faults interfering with performance including weaving; side-winding; crossing-over; high knee action; paddling; and short, choppy movement, should be severely penalized.

Temperament—True Labrador Retriever temperament is as much a hallmark of the breed as the "otter" tail. The ideal disposition is one of a kindly, outgoing, tractable nature; eager to please and non-aggressive towards man or animal. The Labrador has much that appeals to people; his gentle ways, intelligence

Don't underestimate the importance of pigmentation in a puppy. Sometimes pigmentation darkens, sometimes not.

and adaptability make him an ideal dog. Aggressiveness towards humans or other animals, or any evidence of shyness in an adult should be severely penalized.

DISQUALIFICATIONS

1. Any deviation from the height prescribed in the Standard.
2. A thoroughly pink nose or one lacking in any pigment.
3. Eye rims without pigment.
4. Docking or otherwise altering the length or natural carriage of the tail.
5. Any other color or a combination of colors other than black, yellow or chocolate as described in the Standard.
Approval Date: February 12, 1994
Effective Date: March 31, 1994

CARING for Your Labrador Retriever

An all too frequent cause of death in Labradors is heat stroke. The breed has been genetically programmed to survive and thrive in icy Atlantic gales. Dogs do not have body sweat glands and have only a few in their paw pads. Their main cooling device is panting. Humans rarely, if ever, are aware of the great increase in heat and humidity at 24 inches above the ground.

Normal canine temperature is 101.5°F. A Labrador tongue is encyclopedic; learn to read it. Memorize the tongue color when the dog is at rest. As a Lab begins to get warm the tongue will extend forward, darkening slightly. If the tongue hangs far out to the side and is a deep purple, wet the dog's whole body, especially the head and groin area. If there are any abnormalities in the Lab's behavior, race to the closest vet's office. During the cooling process do not allow the dog's temperature to drop below 103°F. Once below 103°F the temperature descent may well become uncontrollable and the dog can die of hypothermia.

"Silent Killers" are heartworms, erhlichiosis, Rocky Mountain spotted fever and Lyme disease. Many biting

If your Labrador is acting lethargic, it may be cause for concern. Notify your vet immediately if you think something is amiss.

insects are carriers, varying with the disease. Due to life cycle development of the heartworm, Labradors should stay on heartworm preventative all year, even if the snow is 4 feet deep. If a puppy retains a "pot belly" even when hungry, check for worms. Heavy infestations are also associated with pale gums. Follow the veterinarian's advice for the geographic area.

The deer tick is the most common carrier of Lyme disease. Photo courtesy of Virbac Laboratories, Inc. Fort Worth, Texas.

On very hot days it is a good idea to take your puppy for a swim to keep him cool.

INHERITED DISEASES

Fortunately, many of the listed diseases and disorders are very rare. A few, unhappily for both Labrador and owner, are all too common.

Missing Teeth:
Cleft Palate—Fissure in roof of mouth, may include lip.
Esophageal Achalsia—Inability to swallow.

Blood:
Hemophilia—clotting deficiency.

Many disorders are hereditary. The importance of breeding from good parents who have been properly screened cannot be over stressed.

Genitourinary:
Cryptorchism—retention of testicles.
Cystinuria—production cystine crystals/stones in the bladder.

Musculoskeletal:
Hip dysplasia—malformation of hip joint(s).
Elbow dysplasia—malformation of elbow joint(s).
Osteochondrosis dissecans— thickened, fissured joint cartilage.
Type II myopathy—deficiency of type II muscle fibers.
Bilateral carpal subluxation—extreme bending of the carpus.
Craniomandibular osteopathy—excessive bone growth on jaw.
Dwarfism—undersized.
Achondroplasia—a form of dwarfism, possible eye disease associated.
Polydactly—rear dew claws.

Nervous System:
Epilepsy—seizures.
Narcolepsy—inappropriate, uncontrolled daytime sleep.
Cataplexy—sudden, complete loss of muscle tone, associated with narcolepsy.

Ocular:
Cataracts—opacity of the eye lens.
Central progressive retinal atrophy—degeneration of

central portion of retina in primary stage.

Distichiasis—eye lash abnormality, may cause scarring of cornea.

Entropion—inverted eye lid.

Ectropion—out turning eye lid, puppies may outgrow.

Luxation of lens—dislocation of lens, may be glaucoma related.

Progressive retinal atrophy—progressing degeneration of retina.

Retinal dysplasia—loose spots/folds in the retina.

Retinal dysplasia, focal/geographic/detachment with skeletal defects—may be associated with achondroplasic dwarfs.

Skin:

Allergic inhalant dermatitis.

Other Structural Malformations:

Calcinosis circumscripta—chalky material in subcutaneous tissues.

Canine Poisons:

Acetaminophen—use baby aspirin only.

Chocolate—contains theobromine; seizures or death may occur.

Alcohol—livers cannot process; possible brain damage.

Antifreeze—irresistible, tastes sweet, deadly in smallest amounts.

Rat poisons. Continuous toilet cleaners—highly

Your pet Labrador should not eat the same foods as you do. Certain foods will cause drastic gastric upsets in your pet.

There are many things in your yard that may be harmful to your Labrador Retriever, such as common garden plants or lawn fertilizers.

suspected carcinogen.

Phenol—chemical used to treat outdoor wood products.

Common garden plants—check with a nurseryman. Toadstools.

Herbicides; insecticides; pesticides.

Hazards:

Choke collars—remove immediately following training.

Rawhide toys.

Natural bones.

Plastic crates in hot weather.

Hot surfaces in warm weather when training or jogging.

Hose water heated by the sun.

Ant beds when training "sits" or "downs."
Fire ants on training birds.
Hidden stumps, rocks or logs beneath the water
surface.

FEEDING

During a week of mystery, a professional training kennel suffered the disappearance of several padlocks. All personnel were questioned. Even more strangely, on the same weekend one of the Labradors would not eat his food.

*Gumabones®
are safe chew
devices that
your Labrador
will enjoy and
benefit from.*

Knowing food refusal is always a dangerous sign for any Lab, the trainer rushed him to the vet. An abdominal x-ray easily found the cause–all seven padlocks.

Labradors do not normally need that much mineral supplementation. With puppies, follow the breeders instructions. As puppies become rather disinterested in one of their daily meals that meal may be eliminated. To prevent poor eating habits, allow no more than 20 minutes for the Lab to finish a meal, then pick up the pan. Labradors are the personification of gluttony. Self-feeding is not normally recommended, as most Labradors will try to eat all of it at one time. *LV: Pant heavily under the dinner table, food will miraculously appear from all directions.*

Do not give your Labrador natural bones of any kind. A four-month-old Labrador puppy has the jaw

A well-balanced meal served once or twice a day is all your Labrador will require to stay healthy and fit.

power to easily shatter a T-bone. Bone splinters may puncture any part of the alimentary track. There are a great variety of Nylabone® products available that veterinarians recommend as safe and healthy for your dog or puppy to chew on. These don't splinter, chip, or break off in large chunks.

Labradors do not need high protein "gold label" dog food (gold also refers to how much of it will be leaving the owner's pocket). Many veterinary specialists in the orthopedic and radiographic fields recommend a lower protein/calcium food for puppies to avoid growth spurts during which joint damage can be done. Unless they are pulling snow sleds in Alaska or field trialing in other states, adult Labs cannot utilize the extra protein. The unused protein residue causes the kidneys to overwork. Unless prescribed by a veterinarian, food supplements, particularly in excess, do nothing but cause problems by upsetting the balance of nutriments in a good dog food and can actually cause a toxicity. When changing dog foods, do so gradually, giving the dog the opportunity to develop different enzymes to digest the new food. Add not more than ¹/₄ new to ³/₄ present food for a few days, then increase to ¹/₂ new, and then ³/₄ new until the change over is completed. Watch for changes in stools, vomiting or food refusal. The lack of proper enzymes is also why table scraps often upset a Labrador's digestive system. As puppies grow they need an increased amount

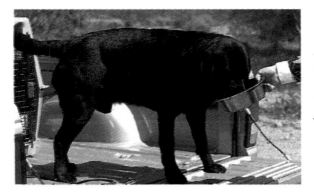

On long trips or outings you must supply your Labrador with plenty of fresh water.

of food, but a decreased number of meals. To find and keep the correct weight for a Labrador puppy or adult use both fingers and eyes. Ribs should be cleanly felt without probing, but not visible. There is nothing more detrimental to a Labrador puppy's joint development than being fat and being fed high protein and calcium.

Labrador Retriever puppies will eat several small meals a day. Gradually, as they grow, the quantity of each meal increases as the number of times they eat decreases.

When calling an area club's Labrador Education number, a proud owner declared his dog was a really big one, he weighed over 100 pounds. The LE person asked how tall the dog was. The owner had never measured the Lab and asked how to do it. When told to measure from the shoulders to the floor, the owner said he would and would call right back. Almost immediately he called again stating the dog was 39 inches tall. The LE said "No way is he purebred, Labs are not that big." After much discussion the LE finally asked "Just how did you measure him?" The answer explained all—"I put his front paws on my shoulders and my wife measured with a tape measure from his shoulders to the floor."

Size is calculated in inches not pounds as weight fluctuates weekly if not daily. Measure with "four on the floor."

GROOMING

The coat of the Labrador may be hosed off or you can allow the dog to go for a swim as an alternative to bathing. Swimming is the very best because of the exercise and pure enjoyment both dog and owner receive. Neither ducks nor Labradors need soap; they both have protective oils. More Labrador coat and skin problems are created by shampooing than money can cure. The correct outer coat of a Labrador is made of coarse, extremely sharp pointed hairs. Even heavy mud will dry and slip off in a matter of a couple of hours. Labradors have a massive shed in the spring, shedding little the rest of the year. The more often a natural bristle brush is used the less hair will be in the butter.

The ears of your Labrador should be checked weekly. If the Labrador is carrying one ear higher than the other, shaking its head, scratching ears often, dragging ears against walls or fencing, check immediately. All dogs with drop ears have a proclivity for wax build-up, swimmer's ear, ear mites, fungus and infections due to a lack of air circulation. Keep the outer portion of the ear clean; leave canal cleaning to the veterinarian.

Your Labrador Retriever requires a lot of play time and exercise.

The nails of your Labrador are too long if a click can be heard on the kitchen floor. Long nails push the toes into abnormal positions, which can eventually lead to arthritis in the affected joints. Learn how to clip nails and at a young age teach the puppy to allow it.

Tartar build-up on teeth is ugly and leads to gum disease. As water supplies and individual Labradors differ, follow your veterinarian's recommendations on how to prevent periodontal disease. Daily brushing is the best answer. Giving your dog regular access to a thermoplastic polymer chew device will prevent calculus build-up as well. Gumabone® products are the only scientifically proven devices that offer the desired protection from tartar and calculus build-up.

As a general grooming practice, a thorough exam should be made of foot pads, between toes, ears, mouth and over all body for cuts or lumps at least once a week. Particular care should be given to mammary glands on bitches and testicles on dogs. Developing this habit will catch any problems at the earliest possible moment.

A puppy should be permitted to exercise at will; it rarely damages itself.

EXERCISE

At a young age allow the puppy or youngster to exercise and rest at will; they rarely damage themselves. Swimming, but not to the point of exhaustion, is the best form of exercise and cleans the Labrador coat. With the Lab's love of water, the owner must carefully watch and make the decision when to stop. Walking will not damage joints, but jogging will. Inveterate joggers need to wait until all of the Labrador's joints have calcified, 18 months is normally safe, then slowly bring the Labrador into running shape. A strong caution: Labradors do not wear "pump up" shoes; their only shock absorbers are their foot pads and those will get sore or burn on hot surfaces.

SPECIAL NEEDS

If a Labrador is remaining outside while its family is at

school and work, there must be continuing shade available as the sun moves. A tub or child's wading pool in a shady spot so the water will not heat will be one of the Lab's favorite locations.

If a Labrador scoots its bottom across the floor or grass, it may have worms, but that is not the cause of the scooting. Canines have vestigial anal glands similar to skunks' active glands. The fluid is not quite as malodorous. Occasionally these glands become full; the owner definitely wants the veterinarian to handle this minor situation. An anal gland problem may become major if the glands become impacted, particularly to the point of rupturing internally. Ruptured glands can cause symptoms exactly like seborrhea or spondylitis. In the

Your Labrador's life can be extended through precautions and routine veterinary care beginning at an early age.

seborrhea type, hair discoloration may be seen on yellows, making a grey shadow up the spinal column with a T across the shoulders. The odor is so strong as it is with true seborrhea that humans cannot stand to stay in the same room with the Labrador. The copycat spondylitis form prohibits males from lifting their legs to urinate; either sex may have difficulty climbing steps or getting in and out of vehicles. A well known veterinary diagnostician was quoted "Whatever you tell me anal glands have done to a dog, I will believe it."

TRAINING Your Labrador Retriever

L abradors are precocious as puppies; they make owners laugh, cry and throw tantrums. The simple fact is either the dogs are trained by their owners or the owners are trained by their dogs. Untrained, the youngsters are extremely strong, active and obnoxious. Without being taught differently, a dog's bad habits last into old age. With Labradors' needs for human touch, they will continually jump in anyone's face or climb into a lap uninvited. Long ago, breeders and owners nicknamed them "LAPradors" and "Lavatory Receivers." *LV: Humans like clean; wash tongue in toilet before giving licks.*

A good Labrador Retriever must know how to hold a bird without damaging or even ruffling the bird's feathers.

Training the puppy before it becomes stronger than the owner is of great benefit to your maintaining pain-free joints and muscles. Teaching humans is far more difficult than training canines. Humans have preconceived ideas, many of their body movements are on "auto-pilot" and must be re-trained. Humans who "can't do that" make excuses for the Labrador's poor behavior, and nag their dogs in training, waiting until after the second or sixth command to make a correction. Labradors are born with "selective hearing," nagging only reinforces it. In an emergency situation there may not be time for more than one command to save the dog's life. Except for aggression work, any training is better than none. Other than for competitive field trials, sending a Labrador away to be trained is not generally recommended. The owner is not being trained, does not learn timing, body language, voice tone control or the dog's reaction in differing situations. The young Labrador will quite often obey the professional trainer well while the owner receives only the "raspberries" and

a large bill. *LV: And just who are you to be telling me what to do?*

Classes at a local obedience club provide socialization and diversion that positively influence the Labrador's mental maturity and concentration. Obedience training greatly increases the bonding love between Labrador and owner. Classes and being a part of the new achievements are great fun for the entire family.

One of the many good reasons to visit the obedience club of choice early is that by observation the owner will learn correct commands to use at home before beginning the actual participation in classes. A "fin and feather" breeder may have taught the puppies "come." If the new owner calls "here," a "huh" may be the only response from a Lab. It is most important to obtain a list of exact commands used if an older Labrador is purchased. Treat and educate untrained adult Labradors

Training your Labrador to retrieve can begin as early as eight weeks of age.

identically to an eight-week-old puppy. Do not skip any steps because of age. Age has nothing to do with experience.

Untitled

"I saw a man who kissed his dog;
A grown up man with a great big dog in obedience.
And this grown up man kissed this great big dog
Right on the nose, right in the ring, between exercises;
In front of his family, the judge, the competition;
And we applauded that great big man
Kissing his dog in front of everybody.
And his great big dog worked like a dog
For the man who kissed his dog."
Author Unknown

Once you introduce your Labrador Retriever to water, it will be difficult to keep him out of it.

Labradors need a job. If the owners do not provide at least one, Labs become very inventive. A particular yellow male champion was notorious for speaking with body language. When HE was ready to come back into the house, HE stood on his hind legs, tapping on the door with his toenails. If HE felt HE had been ignored long enough, HE would slip silently behind his owner and let out a loud "woof!" Food and fluids often approached the ceiling. In training HE decided which was to be HIS last bird. On HIS return to the heel position instead of sitting, HE laid down still holding the bird. When traveling if HE decided it was time to move on, HE would sit in the driver's seat for an hour or more. If that statement failed to bring results, HE would move to plan B and empty everything moveable out of the van. If HIS house was neat, HE never touched a thing. If indeed HIS house was in need of being picked up and a good cleaning, throw

pillows, dirty laundry, various and sundry items would appear in the strangest locations. Just once when HIS owner went on vacation HE stayed with a grandmother, the owner of his sire. The two women breeders had been close friends for years and Grandma was well aware of HIS habits. Immediately upon returning, the owner called to find out if all was well. They chuckled over some of HIS in-house antics and then Grandma said "But darn him, HE put my favorite shorts and T-shirt in the toilet." HIS owner quipped "How long has it been since you washed them?" Laughing, Grandma said "That's not the worst part, HE only put them half way in so they wicked the water out all over the bathroom floor." HIS owner giggled "And how long had it been since you mopped the floor?" HE has not been invited back.

A happy Labrador is one who is kept busy. This Labrador Retriever enjoys playing with his Gumabone® Frisbee® *.

*The trademark Frisbee is used under license from Mattel, Inc., California, USA.

Whole libraries could be filled with the number of books that have been written on obedience and its ultimate extension, retriever field training. There is some information, both common sense and from a retriever training point of view, that bears repeating. Two absolute rules, no compromise: **never lose your temper** and **be consistent.**

Frustrated anger with a child or Labrador is a normal course of events. Displaying the anger is the deciding factor; a dog may be ruined for life. Silently put the Labrador in its crate and plant a petunia, take a cold shower or go to a movie. Being ignored is serious punishment for a Labrador of any age. The basics of dog training are: teach, train, test. Never give a

Your Labrador needs to have a job. If not assigned one, he will go looking for something to do on his own.

command that cannot be enforced. Once a Labrador firmly understands a command but chooses to disobey it, make a correction with, not after, the second command. Never punish a confused dog. Use the Labrador's name before the command. Always set up a training situation to insure success. **Have fun!** Unless an owner is a professional trainer, dog time and training are supposed to be an enjoyable, relaxing sport. It only becomes stressful when the owner sets that attitude. A friend claims bragging rights as his dog is a little ahead, up comes the competitive adrenaline. Perhaps most unfair is to make a new dog walk in the shadow of a previous Labrador. Keep early training happy and positive and take the dog along at its own pace; both Labrador and owner will learn more and progress more quickly. Children cannot learn by attending school once a week, neither can the brightest Labrador. Whichever command is being taught or trained, 3 x 3 are the magic numbers. Three times in a row, three times a day (minimum) will teach without boredom. Practice having the dog respond correctly to different voice levels, including a whisper. Save shouting for distance work and emergencies.

NAMES

Most breeders do not name puppies, using only a happy "come puppy." An easy way to teach a dog its newly chosen name is to add the name at the end — "Come puppy Leo," eventually dropping "puppy" when the Labrador responds to its new name. This is the first example of "stair stepping," which will continue throughout all training. "Stair stepping" utilizes what the Labrador does by instinct or knowledge and builds on it. "No" is the first command taught. The dog's name and the single word "no" are always used, not "Don't do that," or "I'm going to kill you, you ..." "No" accompanied by a thump on the offending part of the Labrador's anatomy is the penalty for the first offense. If the crime is immediately repeated, as will be done by the more bold Labradors, take a firm grip on the scruff of the neck and give a shake, making the "no" considerably louder. The three-time loser goes in its crate for five minutes. Set the kitchen timer. All Labrador owners are intelligent; all intelligent owners use crates. The correct term is crate, not cage.

HOUSEBREAKING

Paper training only gives the dog permission to eliminate inside the house. Pick one door that leads to a fenced yard and can be seen from the greatest area inside the house. During training always use that same door. If the puppy goes near it, take him outside. If a puppy has just awakened from sleep, finished eating, is sniffing along a wall, behind furniture or especially if turning in circles, move fast! If the Labrador was

Although the breeder can initiate housebreaking, the owner is responsible for instilling clean habits.

quicker than you, firmly say "no," pick the puppy up or grip the adult's collar and quickly go out the chosen door. Do not allow the job to be finished inside the house. Carrying the puppy outside will distract him temporarily so be patient and give his immature nervous system time to remind him he did need to go. Take him to the same place he chose before; the scent will also help remind him. Wait until the job is completed before any praise is given or the flow will be interrupted. One Labrador was house trained the old fashioned way by rubbing his nose in "it." For all of his 14 years he eliminated in the house, stuck his nose in "it" and ran for the door. Made sense to him, that is what he was trained to do! Another new owner was quickly trained by her puppy. As part of the pre-Labrador decor, a leather strap with bells attached hung from the kitchen door. Holly, the new puppy, soon learned if she jingled the bells, her owner's response was to open the door. Holly is now the bell ringer for all four Labradors in residence.

COME

The most often made first mistake is calling an off lead Labrador before the "come" command is understood. With no lead, the command cannot be enforced. When this occurs, make the dog look by hand clapping, whistling or some other device, then run in the opposite direction. Labs do not consider "turn about" as fair play, cannot stand being left and will race to the owner. Never for any reason call a Labrador in for correction. The owner is then punishing the dog for obeying the come command. Go

It is easier to teach your Labrador to obey the "come" command if a lead is used.

to the place of infraction and make the correction where the crime occurred; it is good exercise and the Labrador receives the message clearly. If the owner is too tired to make the trip to the location, it is long past time to stop.

STAY VS. STEADY

Contrary to what most all breed obedience books and classes teach, the separate commands for "stay," as in

The command "stay" is already associated with such commands as "sit," "down," "kennel" and "stand."

"sit/stay," or "down/stay," train a Labrador to "stay" in any position until a release command is given. "Sit" means sit until told otherwise, the word "stay" is not necessary. If stay is automatically taught with all positions, it is less confusing for dog and owner. The automatic stay is also associated with the commands "kennel" and "stand." Being "steady," remaining in whatever position commanded, is the most important lesson a Labrador can be taught. It is the equivalent of a safety mechanism on a shotgun. Being steady conflicts with the natural canine instinct to chase prey and a Labrador's strong retrieving instinct. Once understood, a Lab must never be allowed to break a position without permission or a very firm immediate correction. Staying where commanded eliminates the dangers of a Labrador jumping into or in front of a shotgun and bolting out of the house or vehicle into traffic.

THEY ARE NOT ALL PERFECT

Shadow, a.k.a. "I'm going to kill you, you S.O.B.," was one of those Labradors with so much heart that the owner, Carter, had to make him stop when training for retrieving, as Shadow would never quit retrieving by choice. Like his sire, Shadow was a "breaker," with all his training he just could not be steadied. As Carter hunted ducks with a sportswriter for the local newspaper, Shadow became a popular sports figure in the fall with

Remaining steady conflicts with the Labrador's instinct to retrieve. Teaching this command, however, can keep your dog out of danger.

Never use wooden sticks to train. Plastic dummies designed for water training are the better, safer choice.

his antics liberally displayed in Sunday editions. Totally frustrated with Shadow's breaking habits Carter called Ron, a friend and the owner of Shadow's sire. Ron was an avid bird hunter with years of experience; his answer to the problem was "Tie Shadow up on a short lead so he can't break." After the weekend Ron called Carter for a Monday morning replay only to be told that Carter would not talk to him. The following Sunday sports page explained: Carter had clipped Shadow to his belt loop. Just as Carter stood up in the boat and shot, Shadow broke taking Carter and his shotgun over the side, head and gun barrel first into the mud. Later in the season Carter shot a duck, which fell into extremely heavy cover at the edge of the water. Shadow was off swimming high, reached land, tore through the cover never breaking stride, streaked up and disappeared over a hill. From the boat, Carter was using whistles and shouting every command he could think of including the infamous "I'm going to kill you, you SOB." Nothing made Shadow even flick an ear, selective hearing had set in. Unfortunately for Carter, the sportswriter was hunting just around the point where Shadow landed and the whole scenario was observed. One hundred and fifty yards from the water's edge Shadow dived into a heavy clump of briary brush and came out with the wounded duck. The whistles and "cuss" words could still be heard coming across the water. Carter got his prize Wood Duck, but that Sunday's edition featured Shadow as a poster dog with the caption "Conserve Game, Trust Your Dog. See story on page 2."

SIT

Teach sit by placing one hand across the puppy or adult's chest, the other hand across its bottom and tip down into the sit position. This is far more comfortable and quick than fighting the dog's natural resistance to a sudden crush on the top of its rump and far less dangerous to hip joint growth.

KENNEL

The command "kennel" literally means for the dog to get in whatever the owner is touching, be it a crate, car,

dog trailer, boat or run. It is easiest to start training with a crate. Place the puppy inside, leaving the door open, petting and praising. The puppy is not let out until the owner stands up and gives

The command "kennel" means the dog should get in whatever you are touching, such as a doghouse.

An adult Labrador will quickly learn the command "kennel" by luring him to the desired place with pieces of food.

the "come" command. To train an adult Labrador to kennel in a crate, start with a hungry dog. Using small pieces of cheese or hamburger balls, sit in front of the crate allowing the dog to smell and try to take treats from the hand. Make sure the dog is watching and throw one piece of food to the back of the crate while saying "kennel." After several throws of treats, the Lab will be comfortable with the idea. The next step is to place the filled food pan at the back of the crate, repeating "kennel."

RELEASE

Although "OK" is often used as a release word, the best

word to use is the Labrador's own name. If training for hunting, hunt tests or field trials, the release word to send the dog for the bird is its name. That name is specific for one dog only. Consider what would happen if a duck boat contained three Labradors and all three were trained to be released with the word "OK" or to fetch birds with the obsolete command "back." The Labrador already knows its name. Why add another word to have to teach?

Early socialization makes for a friendly and well-mannered Labrador.

A SOCIAL ANIMAL

Socialization is a long dog word for becoming comfortably familiar with new occurrences and happenings. Show and obedience people often have younger puppies with them to stroll around noisy buildings after the show is over, meeting new people, letting the youngsters walk on mats, through gates, in and around crating areas. Outdoor "fun matches" (non-point-giving shows and obedience trials) are great places to socialize, all the other people there are doing the same thing. Outside malls are excellent locations for puppies on lead to meet strangers and become immune to traffic noises. Do be considerate of children and clothing by not letting the Labrador jump up on people. Flooring can have a negative effect on Labradors. Teach the dog to climb up and down stairs; walk across newspaper, shiny spaces, blankets laid on grass, slick floors and metal grids (be careful not to catch a toenail); and ride in elevators

and boats—avoid escalators. Different surfaces are required as part of a Canine Good

Bringing your Labrador to outside "fun matches" is a great way to socialize him.

Citizen title; however, the most important reason for
surface training is to be able to get both the owner and
the dog out of emergency situations. Speed does not
come easily if an 85 pound Labrador has set the brakes.
To fulfill their potential and satisfy instincts, Labradors
need to have the opportunity to be socialized in a greater
area. Careful introduction to non-aggressive dogs is
important as quite often a Lab has to work with other
dogs. Cover, water, training dummies, birds and gun fire
should all be intelligently introduced.

COVER

The word cover is short for ground cover. *LV: The best
cover is in the middle of the human bed.*

City parks, country walks and hunting leases are
places to start Labradors of any age. An owner should
follow along keeping a firm hold on the long lead or
check cord and just let the dog investigate on his own. A
strong "no" is in order for cactus and skunks, but all
Labradors will argue with both at least once.

WATER

If the weather, water or bank is not good enough for
the owner, it is not good enough for a reluctant puppy
or adult Labrador. Set up the situation for success and
safety. In late spring or summer when the water has had
time to warm, wear old tennis shoes, choose a spot with
a gradually sloping bank and shallow water. Walk in with
the Labrador using happy encouragement and he will be
in swimming water before you. Let the Labrador just
enjoy the water the first few times before starting any
training. Don't do water retrieves until the dog is doing
very well on land. Unless a boat or a trained "pickup"
dog is available, do not throw anything in the water that
the trainer is not willing to lose or swim after himself.

TRAINING WITH TRAINING DUMMIES

If nothing else is learned, know when to quit! Quit on

a successful retrieve even if it is only 3 feet long. Read your Labrador; it may be the dog's decreasing speed, the way the head or tail is carried, fooling around about finding or picking up the dummy, just a feeling inside the trainer or the dog lying down with the bird. An Irish Water Spaniel puppy who had one too many thrown for her retrieved from the water beautifully, came half way back, put the bird in tall grass, curled up on top of it and went to sleep. Always put the Labrador away who is begging for more. The second most important observation is to note whether the dog's body is lined up with the dummy or bird or is just the head looking in the correct direction—the drive shaft is not located in the head. Trainers must develop a habit of checking the dog's spinal column clear to the base of the tail. If the body does not line up, move the dog because whatever

When training your Labrador Retriever to retrieve, make sure the situation is set up for success and safety.

direction the spinal column is in will be the course of running regardless of where the bird fell. Dummies are not toys; a Labrador should not be allowed to play with them. The dummies will cease to be special and the play attitude may start a multitude of bad habits. Start with plastic knobbies, they are easier to see and the least favorite of Labradors. If started on canvas, or worse, birds, the dogs may refuse to ever pick up anything else. To get the dog's attention, the trainer or thrower should call "hey, hey, hey" as the dummy is being swung around and thrown.

BIRDS

One of the best ways to introduce birds to an inexperienced Labrador is to let the dog watch an advanced retriever work. Have the novice close enough to be able to both smell and see the bird being retrieved, 6 feet from the bird would be a good distance. Another "stair step" is attaching game bird wings to training dummies with large rubber bands or duct tape. Start with one wing, adding more as the dog progresses. The first time a Labrador gets a whole bird of its own to first smell then retrieve from a short distance, use a cold dead bird. Live birds may scare an unsure dog or bring on too strong a reaction in the very bold Labrador. Live birds may be used to resurrect the "prey chase" instinct in the rare Labrador who shows little interest in retrieving.

This pup's training has begun, and he has a real taste for it!

GUNS

A gunshot hurts dogs' sensitive ears and can frighten the less bold Labrador of any age if not properly introduced. Once the Labrador is running out to retrieve at 30 yards, the time has come to "stair step." Have the thrower add one shot from a blank pistol in the middle of the "hey, hey, heys." Practice at that level of noise until only the shot is used to get the dog's attention. Next use a 4/10 or 20 gauge, finally finishing with a 12 gauge, but only at a distance. Each training session move the gun slightly closer, watching

If your Labrador is accustomed to loud noises, such as a gunshot, at an early age, he will not be shy of these as an adult.

The correct form for sending your Labrador.

97

the dog's reaction, until the gun can be fired next to the dog. A dummy or bird must be thrown with each shot.

WHEN NOT TO RETRIEVER TRAIN

In all the following time periods keep up the obedience training, but slow down or temporarily stop retriever training. When a puppy starts cutting its adult teeth and the baby teeth are loose making the gums sore, the puppy may associate the increase in mouth pain with the dummy or bird. Puppies become stubborn at this time. Puppies have pre-puberty syndrome (PPS) when huge hormone surges occur in their bodies. Time will vary with the individual dogs, but the 9th to the 11th months are common. Although first seasons in bitches are the worst, most bitches have their minds on other things whenever in season (PMS). Both syndromes will produce strange reactions from being afraid of everything to total disinterest in retrieving.

BUILDING HOLES

Labradors are not the only hole builders, owner/trainers can dig some beauties. This term refers to small mistakes made early in training or the ignoring of minor bad habits in the dog that become enormous when extensions are applied. Dogs may play chase or tug-o-war with each other, but never with a human. Retrieve means to bring back. If humans chase a Lab, the retrieving

If you are going to play chase with your Labrador, make sure the dog chases you, not the reverse, as it can harm the retrieving instinct.

instinct is usually destroyed as a new fun game has taken its place. If chase must be played, make sure the Labrador chases the human, not the reverse. Be cautious about very small children playing this game. No matter how much dogs are anthropomorphised by humans they are still canines and as such have strong prey chase instincts and may accidentally hurt a young child. Labradors are to have soft, gentle mouths and deliver game readily to hand. What does tug-o-war teach them?

Always correct your Labrador immediately for a wrong act, such as jumping up. If left unnoticed the Labrador Retriever will continue to misbehave.

Temporary silence is permanently golden. If the excited owner gives praise just as a puppy is about to pick up a dummy or bird, it will distract the puppy enough that the retrieve will be forgotten and the puppy will run to the owner. When the pup has picked up, start backing up, giving the "come" command. When the puppy delivers to hand, give lavish, foolish praise—who cares what the neighbors think. "Short hunting" is usually caused by the owner training alone. Any one person can only throw a dummy or bird so far and is usually very consistent in the distance. Labradors quickly learn to go that distance and not a yard farther. Enlist family members to throw or train with a friend, taking turns throwing for each others dogs so that the distances may be varied. Recall refusal means that the dog cannot find the bird, but refuses to come in without it no matter how many whistles or commands the trainer gives. Persistence is great in a Labrador, but this is disobedience. The one thing the trainer should never do is tell the thrower to pitch out another bird so the dog will come back. That is rewarding the disobedience. If a "come" whistle or command has been given and disobeyed, the trainer must walk out to the dog, physically and none too comfortably take the dog back to the line (starting point) and ask the thrower to pick up the bird. If the "come" command or whistle has not been given, then the trainer may ask the thrower to "hey, hey, hey" and throw out another bird so that the retrieve may be successfully completed. No disobedience is involved as no command has been given. Be wary of helping too quickly or often, Labs are "lazy-smart." Avoidance of bad habits can be achieved by allowing no "off check cord" retrieving work until basic obedience is well rehearsed (it is never complete). With a check cord the trainer has full control and can gently enforce commands, ensuring success. Later bad habits may be avoided or corrected by having periodic refresher courses on all basic obedience combined with quick drills just before going to retrieve.

Avoid bad habits by not allowing "off check cord" retrieving work until basic obedience is instilled.

TRAINING TIPS

Whether the owner/trainer and thrower are setting up a training situation or the owner is among the group when all handlers are called to the line at a hunt test or field trial, the owner should squat down and watch the bird or dummy fall from the Labrador's line of sight. As with heat and humidity, it is entirely different down there. Branches, bushes, knolls and water glare will appear that could not be seen from above.

The kids played tug-o-war and now the dog is freezing (squeezing and refusing to release) on the bird the owner

A properly trained Labrador Retriever will hold the retrieve in his mouth until given the command to drop it in his trainer's hand.

planned to eat at Christmas dinner. The owner should stand with his knees facing the dog's left shoulder, left hand on, but not pulling, the bird while giving the release command of "drop." The owner reaches across the Labrador's back with his right hand, firmly grips the flap (the 2- to 3-inch long layer of skin that superficially connects the body to the front of the thigh) and lifts up. The dog is surprised and may yelp, but eases the crush on the bird; the owner then should quickly take the bird and give a mild "good dog." The dog cannot associate the discomfort with the owner because he knows the owner is on the other side, nor with the bird because his mouth did not hurt. Hard mouth and freezing on the bird are two of the hardest habits to break.

To extend the distances of the retrieves, the owner/ trainer and dog back up, not the thrower. If the thrower moves farther out, then the novice dog must drive through the very recent bird scents. Those scents would stop many experienced dogs. As the dog is going out for the first retrieve, the owner backs up 6 to 10 feet and receives the bird in the new location. The dog is also sent from this new location and the process is repeated. In just three retrieves the distance can be extended by 30 feet.

When land and water singles have been well established at a variety of distances, the time has come to introduce doubles. The Labrador must mark and remember where two birds fell. Find an outside corner of fence, stand within one stride of the corner with the dog sitting at heel. At very short distances throw the first bird to the left of the corner, then the second bird to the right of the corner. Send the dog after the first bird thrown. A Labrador is no fool, he is going to try to pick up both birds in one trip. Step

The Labrador shows enthusiasm with each and every retrieve.

forward, take hold of the collar, swing him back to the original position take the bird and quickly send him for the second. At first he may be confused, but a little help and encouragement will solve it.

Blinds are the toughest. The dog has not seen a bird fall and has nothing but trust in the owner who is telling him there really is a bird out there. Build the trust early by lining the puppy to his food pan. On the patio or in the back yard, put the puppy in the sit position with the food pan just 2 or 3 feet away. Say "line," the puppy's name and release him to run for dinner. One meal a day extend the food pan farther away eventually under bushes or another hidden site. Always place the spinal column in the correct direction.

The Labrador has natural retrieving instincts that are just begging to be developed.

Hunt-ups are nice strolls through park paths or across pastures, the difference being the route has been salted with birds. At the start and periodically during the walk use the command "hunt." Lavish praise and hugs are given as each treasure is discovered and delivered.

Perspective and confidence can be developed by a simple training setup. The thrower stands on the pitcher's mound and throws only to homeplate. The owner/trainer sends the dog from different points around the imaginary baseball field except second base. From second base the thrower's body would block the view of the fall. Birds and scents all stay in the same area and the dog sees the falls from all possible angles.

THE RAINBOW BRIDGE

Just this side of heaven is a place called Rainbow Bridge. When an animal dies that has been especially close to someone here, that pet goes to Rainbow Bridge. There are meadows and hills for all of the special friends so they can run and play together. There is plenty of food, water and sunshine, and our friends are warm and comfortable. All of the animals who have been ill and old are restored to health and vigor; those who were hurt or maimed are made whole and strong again, just as we remember them in our dreams of days and times gone by. The animals are happy and content except for one small thing: they each miss someone very special to them who had to be left behind. They all run and play together, but the day comes when one suddenly stops and looks in the distance. His bright eyes are intent; his eager body begins to quiver. Suddenly he begins to run from the group, flying over green grass, his legs carrying him faster and faster. You have been spotted, and when you and your special friend meet, you cling together in joyous reunion, never to be parted again. The happy kisses rain upon your face, your hands again caress the beloved head, and you look once more into the trusting eyes of your pet, so long gone from your life, but never absent from your heart. Then you cross the Rainbow Bridge together...
Author Unknown

For Tad, my son, and Shammy, my first champion, who wait at the Rainbow Bridge.

Inevitably...Mother Nature may have used her sense of humor when inventing Labrador Retrievers, but she painted no more beautiful portrait than that of an old campaigner, the frost of age on his muzzle, still as a statue in boat or blind, his eyes only moving like silent pickpockets across the skies.

Head study of Ch. Wyndcalls Rampart.

SPORT of Purebred Dogs

Welcome to the exciting and sometimes frustrating sport of dogs. No doubt you are trying to learn more about dogs or you wouldn't be deep into this book. This section covers the basics that may entice you, further your knowledge and help you to understand the dog world. If you decide to give showing, obedience or any other dog activities a try, then I suggest you seek further help from the appropriate source.

Dog showing has been a very popular sport for a long time and has been taken quite seriously by some. Others only enjoy it as a hobby.

The Kennel Club in England was formed in 1859, the American Kennel Club was established in 1884 and the Canadian Kennel Club was formed in 1888. The purpose of these clubs was to register purebred dogs and maintain their Stud Books. In the beginning, the concept of registering dogs was not readily accepted. More than 36 million dogs have been enrolled in the AKC Stud Book since its inception in 1888. Presently the kennel clubs not only register dogs but adopt and enforce rules and regulations governing dog shows, obedience trials and field trials. Over the years they have fostered and encouraged interest in the health and welfare of the purebred dog. They routinely donate funds to veterinary research for study on genetic disorders.

Below are the addresses of the kennel clubs in the United States, Great Britain and Canada.

The American Kennel Club
51 Madison Avenue
New York, NY 10010
(Their registry is located at: 5580 Centerview Drive, STE 200, Raleigh, NC 27606-3390)

The Kennel Club

1 Clarges Street
Piccadilly, London, WIY 8AB, England

The Canadian Kennel Club
111 Eglinton Avenue
East Toronto, Ontario M6S 4V7
Canada

Today there are numerous
activities that are enjoyable for
both the dog and the handler.
Some of the activities include
conformation showing,
obedience competition, tracking,
agility, the Canine Good Citizen
Certificate, and a wide range of
instinct tests that vary from breed
to breed. Where you start
depends upon your goals which
early on may not be readily
apparent.

Agility is just one of the many activities in which Labradors demonstrate their athletic and competitive prowess.

CONFORMATION

Conformation showing is our oldest dog show sport.
This type of showing is based on the dog's appearance—
that is his structure, movement and attitude. When
considering this type of showing, you need to be aware
of your breed's standard and be able to evaluate your
dog compared to that standard. The breeder of your
puppy or other experienced breeders would be good
sources for such an evaluation. Puppies can go through
lots of changes over a period of time. I always say most
puppies start out as promising hopefuls and then after
maturing may be disappointing as show candidates.
Even so this should not deter them from being excellent
pets.

Usually conformation training classes are offered by
the local kennel or obedience clubs. These are
excellent places for training puppies. The puppy should
be able to walk on a lead before entering such a class.
Proper ring procedure and technique for posing

(stacking) the dog will be demonstrated as well as gaiting the dog. Usually certain patterns are used in the ring such as the triangle or the "L." Conformation class, like the PKT class, will give your youngster the opportunity to socialize with different breeds of dogs and humans too.

It takes some time to learn the routine of conformation showing. Usually one starts at the puppy matches which may be AKC Sanctioned or Fun Matches. These matches are generally for puppies from two or three months to a year old, and there may be classes for the adult over the age of 12 months. Similar to point shows, the classes are divided by sex and after *A future show dog must be accustomed to walking on a lead, being among people, and being handled by strangers.* completion of the classes in that breed or variety, the class winners compete for Best of Breed or Variety. The winner goes on to compete in the Group and the Group winners compete for Best in Match. No championship points are awarded for match wins.

A few matches can be great training for puppies even though there is no intention to go on showing. Matches enable the puppy to meet new people and be handled by a stranger—the judge. It is also a change of environment, which broadens the horizon for both dog and handler. Matches and other dog activities boost the confidence of the handler and especially the younger handlers.

Earning an AKC championship is built on a point system, which is different from Great Britain. To become an AKC Champion of Record the dog must earn 15 points. The number of points earned each time depends upon the number of dogs in competition. The number of points available at each show depends upon the breed, its sex and the location of the show. The United States is divided into ten AKC zones. Each zone has its own set of points. The purpose of the zones is to try to equalize the points available from breed to breed and area to area.The AKC adjusts the point scale annually.

The number of points that can be won at a show are between one and five. Three-, four- and five-point wins are considered majors. Not only does the dog need 15 points won under three different judges, but those points must

include two majors under two different judges. Canada also works on a point system but majors are not required.

Junior Showmanship

The Junior Showmanship Class is a wonderful way to build self confidence even if there are no aspirations of staying with the dog-show game later in life. Frequently, Junior Showmanship becomes the background of those who become successful exhibitors/handlers in the future. In some instances it is taken very seriously, and success is measured in terms of wins. The Junior Handler is judged solely on his ability and skill in presenting his dog. The dog's conformation is not to be considered by the judge. Even so the condition and grooming of the dog may be a reflection upon the handler.

Obedience training allows the owner and dog to develop a closeness through working together.

Usually the matches and point shows include different classes. The Junior Handler's dog may be entered in a breed or obedience class and even shown by another person in that class. Junior Showmanship classes are usually divided by age and perhaps sex. The age is determined by the handler's age on the day of the show. The classes are:

Novice Junior for those at least ten and under 14 years of age who at time of entry closing have not won three first places in a Novice Class at a licensed or member show.

Novice Senior for those at least 14 and under 18 years of age who at the time of entry closing have not won three first places in a Novice Class at a licensed or member show.

Open Junior for those at least ten and under 14 years of age who at the time of entry closing have won at least three

Aside from the dazzling trophies it awards, dog showing is rewarding in many ways for both owner and dog.

110

first places in a Novice Junior Showmanship Class at a licensed or member show with competition present.

Open Senior for those at least 14 and under 18 years of age who at time of entry closing have won at least three first places in a Novice Junior Showmanship Class at a licensed or member show with competition present.

Junior Handlers must include their AKC Junior Handler number on each show entry. This needs to be obtained from the AKC.

CANINE GOOD CITIZEN

The AKC sponsors a program to encourage dog owners to train their dogs. Local clubs perform the pass/fail tests, and dogs who pass are awarded a Canine Good Citizen Certificate. Proof of vaccination is required at the time of participation. The test includes:

1. Accepting a friendly stranger.
2. Sitting politely for petting.
3. Appearance and grooming.
4. Walking on a loose leash.
5. Walking through a crowd.
6. Sit and down on command/staying in place.
7. Come when called.
8. Reaction to another dog.
9. Reactions to distractions.
10. Supervised separation.

If more effort was made by pet owners to accomplish these exercises, fewer dogs would be cast off to the humane shelter.

OBEDIENCE

Obedience is necessary, without a doubt, but it can also become a wonderful hobby or even an obsession. In my opinion, obedience classes and competition can provide wonderful companionship, not only with your dog but with your classmates or fellow competitors. It is always gratifying to discuss your dog's problems with others who have had similar experiences. The AKC acknowledged Obedience around 1936, and it has changed tremendously even though many of the exercises are basically the same. Today, obedience competition is just that—very competitive. Even so, it is possible for every obedience exhibitor to come home a winner (by earning qualifying scores) even though he/she may not earn a placement in the class.

Most of the obedience titles are awarded after earning three qualifying scores (legs) in the appropriate class under three different judges. These classes offer a perfect score of 200, which is extremely rare. Each of the class exercises has its own point value. A leg is earned after receiving a score of at least 170 and at least 50 percent of the points available in each exercise. The titles are:

Companion Dog–CD

This is called the Novice Class and the exercises are:

1. Heel on leash and figure 8		40 points
2. Stand for examination		30 points
	3. Heel free	40 points
Marsh Dak's	4. Recall	30 points
Shooting Star, CD,	5. Long sit–one minute	30 points
demonstrating	6. Long down–three minutes	30 points
the down	Maximum total score	200 points
command.		

Companion Dog Excellent–CDX
This is the Open Class and the exercises are:

1. Heel off leash and figure 8	40 points
2. Drop on recall	30 points
3. Retrieve on flat	20 points
4. Retrieve over high jump	30 points
5. Broad jump	20 points
6. Long sit–three minutes (out of sight)	30 points
7. Long down–five minutes (out of sight)	30 points
Maximum total score	200 points

Utility Dog–UD
The Utility Class exercises are:

1. Signal Exercise	40 points
2. Scent discrimination-Article 1	30 points
3. Scent discrimination-Article 2	30 points
4. Directed retrieve	30 points
5. Moving stand and examination	30 points
6. Directed jumping	40 points
Maximum total score	200 points

After achieving the UD title, you may feel inclined to go after the UDX and/or OTCh. The UDX (Utility Dog Excellent) title went into effect in January 1994. It is not easily attained. The title requires qualifying simultaneously ten times in Open B and Utility B but not necessarily at consecutive shows.

The OTCh (Obedience Trial Champion) is awarded after

This yellow Labrador easily clears the bar jump at an agility trial.

the dog has earned his UD and then goes on to earn 100 championship points, a first place in Utility, a first place in Open and another first place in either class. The placements must be won under three different judges at all-breed obedience trials. The points are determined by the number of dogs competing in the Open B and Utility B classes. The OTCh title precedes the dog's name.

Basic obedience training assures you of a mannerly and polite Labrador wherever you go.

Obedience matches (AKC Sanctioned, Fun, and Show and Go) are usually available. Usually they are sponsored by the local obedience clubs. When preparing an obedience dog for a title, you will find matches very helpful. Fun Matches and Show and Go Matches are more lenient in allowing you to

Marsh Dak's Shooting Star, CD performing at obedience trial. Owner, Dianne L. Schlemmer.

make corrections in the ring. I frequently train (correct) in the ring and inform the judge that I would like to do so and to please mark me "exhibition." This means that I will not be eligible for any prize. This type of training is usually very necessary for the Open and Utility Classes. AKC Sanctioned Obedience Matches do not allow corrections in the ring since they must abide by the AKC Obedience Regulations. If you are interested in showing in obedience, then you should contact the AKC for a copy of the Obedience Regulations.

TRACKING

Tracking is officially classified obedience, but I feel it should have its own category. There are three tracking titles available: Tracking Dog (TD), Tracking Dog Excellent (TDX), Variable Surface Tracking (VST). If all three tracking titles are obtained, then the dog officially becomes a CT (Champion Tracker). The CT will go in front of the dog's name.

A TD may be earned anytime and does not have to follow the other obedience titles. There are many exhibitors that prefer tracking to obedience, and there are others like myself that do both. In my experience with small dogs, I prefer to earn the CD and CDX before attempting tracking. My reasoning is that small dogs are closer to the mat in the obedience rings and therefore it's too easy to put the nose down and sniff. Tracking encourages sniffing. Of course this depends on the dog. I've had some dogs that tracked around the ring and others (TDXs) who wouldn't think of sniffing in the ring.

Tracking Dog–TD

A dog must be certified by an AKC tracking judge that he is ready to perform in an AKC test. The AKC can provide the names of tracking judges in your area that you can contact for certification. Depending on where you live, you may have to travel a distance if there is no local tracking judge. The certification track will be equivalent to a regular AKC track. A regulation track must be 440 to 500 yards long with at least two right-angle turns out in the open. The track will be aged 30 minutes to two hours. The handler has two starting flags at the beginning of the track to indicate the direction started. The dog works on a harness and 40-foot lead and must work at least 20 feet in front of the handler. An article (either a dark glove or wallet) will be dropped at the end of the track, and the dog must indicate it but not necessarily retrieve it.

People always ask me what the dog tracks. In my opinion, initially, the beginner on the short-aged track tracks the tracklayer. Eventually the dog learns to track the disturbed vegetation and learns to differentiate between tracks. Getting started with tracking requires reading the AKC regulations and a good book on tracking plus finding other tracking enthusiasts. I like to work on the buddy system. That is—we lay tracks for each other so we can practice blind tracks. It is possible to train on your own, but if you are a beginner, it is a lot more entertaining to track with a buddy. Tracking is my favorite dog sport. It's rewarding seeing the dog use his natural ability.

The even-tempered Labrador has a keen nose and is frequently used by police and government agencies to detect drugs and arson suspicions.

Tracking Dog Excellent—TDX

The TDX track is 800 to 1000 yards long and is aged three to five hours. There will be five to seven turns. An article is left at the starting flag, and three other articles must be indicated on the track. There is only one flag at

the start, so it is a blind start. Approximately one and a half hours after the track is laid, two tracklayers will cross over the track at two different places to test the dog's ability to stay with the original track. There will be at least two obstacles on the track such as a change of cover, fences, creeks, ditches, etc. The dog must have a TD before entering a TDX. There is no certification required for a TDX.

Variable Surface Tracking–VST

This test came into effect September 1995. The dog must have a TD earned at least six months prior to entering this test. The track is

This black Labrador is pictured acing the A-frame at an agility trial.

600 to 800 yards long and shall have a minimum of three different surfaces. Vegetation shall be included along with two areas devoid of vegetation such as concrete, asphalt, gravel, sand, hard pan or mulch. The areas devoid of vegetation shall comprise at least one-third to one-half of the track. The track is aged three to five hours. There will be four to eight turns and four numbered articles including one leather, one plastic, one metal and one fabric dropped on the track. There is one starting flag. The handler will work at least 10 feet from the dog.

Tracking Championship–TC

This is awarded when a dog has achieved all three titles.

AGILITY

Agility was first introduced by John Varley in England at the Crufts Dog Show, February 1978, but Peter Meanwell, competitor and judge, actually developed the idea. It was officially recognized in the early '80s. Agility is extremely popular in England and Canada and growing in popularity in the U.S. The AKC acknowledged agility in August 1994. Dogs must be at least 12 months of age to be entered. It is a fascinating sport that the dog, handler and spectators enjoy to the utmost. Agility is a spectator sport! The dog performs off lead. The handler either runs with his dog or positions himself on the course and directs his dog with verbal and hand signals over a timed course over or through a variety of obstacles including a time out or pause. One of the main drawbacks to agility is finding a place to train. The obstacles take up a lot of

space and it is very time consuming to put up and take down courses.

The titles earned at AKC agility trials are Novice Agility Dog (NAD), Open Agility Dog (OAD), Agility Dog Excellent (ADX), and Master Agility Excellent (MAX). In order to acquire an agility title, a dog must earn a qualifying score in its respective class on three separate occasions under two different judges. The MAX will be awarded after earning ten qualifying scores in the Agility Excellent Class.

PERFORMANCE TESTS

During the last decade the American Kennel Club has promoted performance tests—those events that test the different breeds' natural abilities. This type of event encourages a handler to devote even more time to his dog and retain the natural instincts of his breed heritage. It is an important part of the wonderful world of dogs.

This Labrador and his English Springer Spaniel friend are practicing retrieves in the water.

Hunting Titles

For retrievers, pointing breeds and spaniels. Titles offered are Junior Hunter (JH), Senior Hunter (SH), and Master Hunter (MH).

Flushing Spaniels Their primary purpose is to hunt, find, flush and return birds to hand as quickly as possible in a pleasing and obedient manner. The entrant must be at least six months of age and dogs with limited registration or ILP are eligible. Game used are pigeons, pheasants, and quail.

Retrievers Limited registration or ILP retrievers are eligible to compete in Hunting Tests. The purpose of a Hunting Test for retrievers is to test the merits of and

The Labrador shows a strong desire to hunt at an early age.

evaluate the abilities of retrievers in the field in order to determine their suitability and ability as hunting companions. They are expected to retrieve any type of game bird, pheasants, ducks, pigeons, guinea hens and quail.

Pointing Breeds Are eligible at six months of age, and dogs with limited registration or ILP are permitted. They must show a keen desire to hunt; be bold and independent; have a fast, yet attractive, manner of hunting; and demonstrate intelligence not only in seeking objectives but also in the ability to find game. They must establish point, and in the more advanced tests they need to be steady to wing and must remain in position until the bird is shot or they are released.

A Senior Hunter must retrieve. A Master Hunter must honor. The judges and the marshal are permitted to ride horseback during the test, but all handling must be done on foot.

GENERAL INFORMATION

Obedience, tracking and agility allow the purebred dog with an Indefinite Listing Privilege (ILP) number or a limited registration to be exhibited and earn titles. Application must be made to the AKC for an ILP number.

The American Kennel Club publishes a monthly *Events* magazine that is part of the *Gazette*, their official journal for the sport of purebred dogs. The *Events* section lists upcoming shows and the secretary or superintendent for them. The majority of the conformation shows in the U.S. are overseen by licensed superintendents. Generally the entry closing date is approximately two-and-a-half weeks before the actual show. Point shows are fairly expensive, while the match shows cost about one third of the point show entry fee. Match shows usually take entries the day of the show but some are pre-entry. The best way to find match show information is through your local kennel club. Upon asking, the AKC can provide you with a list of superintendents, and you can write and ask to be put on their mailing lists.

Labrador Retriever "Missouri River Lady" in Junior Hunter Test with Pete Russos.

Obedience trial and tracking test information is available through the AKC. Frequently these events are not superintended, but put on by the host club. Therefore you would make the entry with the event's secretary.

As you have read, there are numerous activities you can share with your dog. Regardless what you do, it does take teamwork. Your dog can only benefit from your attention and training.

Labradors have proven to excel in all types of work, including search and rescue. This is "Kiwi" digging for a buried avalanche victim.

TRAVELING with Your Dog

The earlier you start traveling with your new puppy or dog, the better. He needs to become accustomed to traveling. However, some dogs are nervous riders and become carsick easily. It is helpful if he starts with an empty stomach. Do not despair, as it will go better if you continue taking him with you on short fun rides. How would you feel if every time you rode in the car you stopped at the doctor's for an injection? You would soon dread that nasty car. Older dogs that tend to get carsick may have more of a problem adjusting to traveling. Those dogs that are having a serious problem may benefit from some medication prescribed by the veterinarian.

Do give your dog a chance to relieve himself before getting into the car. It is a good idea to be prepared for a clean up with a leash, paper towels, bag and terry cloth towel.

The safest place for your dog is in a fiberglass crate, although close confinement can promote carsickness in some dogs. If your dog is nervous you can try letting him ride on the seat next to you or in someone's lap.

An alternative to the crate would be to use a car harness made for dogs and/or a safety strap attached to the harness

Do not let your Labrador ride in the back of a pick-up truck unless he is in a crate. Labs have been known to jump over the side even on short leads.

or collar. Whatever you do, do not let your dog ride in the back of a pickup truck. I've seen trucks stop quickly and, even though the dog was tied, it fell out and was dragged.

I do occasionally let my dogs ride loose with me because I really enjoy their companionship, but in all honesty they are safer in their crates. I have a friend whose van rolled in an accident but his dogs, in their fiberglass crates, were not injured nor did they escape.

Better boarding kennels are equipped with long runs to exercise your Labrador Retriever properly while you are away.

Fresh water is vital to your Labrador while you are out on day trips or vacationing.

Another advantage of the crate is that it is a safe place to leave him if you need to run into the store. Otherwise you wouldn't be able to leave the windows

down. Keep in mind that while many dogs are overly protective in their crates, this may not be enough to deter dognappers. In some states it is against the law to leave a dog in the car unattended.

Never leave a dog loose in the car wearing a collar and leash. I have known more than one dog that has killed himself by hanging. Do not let him put his head out an open window. Foreign debris can be blown into his eyes. When leaving your dog unattended in a car, consider the temperature. It can take less than five minutes to reach temperatures over 100 degrees Fahrenheit.

TRIPS

Perhaps you are taking a trip. Give consideration to what is best for your dog—traveling with you or boarding. When traveling by car, van or motor

Crates are a safe way for your dog to travel. The fiberglass crates are safer for travel but the metal crates allow more air.

home, you need to think ahead about locking your vehicle. In all probability you have many valuables in the car and do not wish to leave it unlocked. Perhaps most valuable and not replaceable is your dog. Give thought to securing your vehicle and providing adequate ventilation for him. Another consideration for you when traveling with your dog is medical problems that may arise and little inconveniences, such as exposure to external parasites. Some areas of the country are quite flea infested. You may want to carry flea spray with you. This is even a good idea when staying in motels. Quite possibly you are not the only occupant of the room.

An exercise pen is great for traveling with your Labrador. It is easy to set up and allows your dog freedom it wouldn't have if attached to a leash.

Unbelievably many motels and even hotels do allow canine guests, even some very first-class ones. Gaines Pet Foods Corporation publishes *Touring With Towser*, a directory of domestic hotels and motels that accommodate guests with dogs. Their address is Gaines TWT, PO Box 5700, Kankakee, IL, 60902. I would recommend you call ahead to any motel that you may be considering and see if they accept pets. Sometimes it is necessary to pay a deposit against room damage. Of course you are more likely to gain accommodations for a small dog than a large dog. Also the management feels reassured when you mention that your dog will be crated. Since my dogs tend to bark when I leave the room, I leave the TV on nearly full blast to deaden the noises outside that tend to encourage my dogs to bark. If you do travel with your dog, take along plenty of baggies so that you can clean up after him. When we all do our share in cleaning up, we make it possible for motels to continue accepting our pets. As a matter of fact, you should practice cleaning up everywhere you take your dog.

Depending on where your are traveling, you may need

an up-to-date health certificate issued by your veterinarian. It is good policy to take along your dog's medical information, which would include the name, address and phone number of your veterinarian, vaccination record, rabies certificate, and any medication he is taking.

AIR TRAVEL

When traveling by air, you need to contact the airlines to check their policy. Usually you have to make arrangements up to a couple of weeks in advance for traveling with your dog. The airlines require your dog to travel in an airline approved fiberglass crate. Usually these can be purchased through the airlines but they are also readily available in most pet-supply stores. If your dog is not accustomed to a crate, then it is a good idea to get him acclimated to it before your

Crates make a car ride safe for both driver and Labrador.

trip. The day of the actual trip you should withhold water about one hour ahead of departure and no food for about 12 hours. The airlines generally have temperature restrictions, which do not allow pets to travel if it is either too cold or too hot. Frequently these restrictions are based on the temperatures at the departure and arrival airports. It's best to inquire about a health certificate. These usually need to be issued within ten days of departure. You should arrange for non-stop, direct flights and if a commuter plane should be involved, check to see if it will carry dogs. Some don't. The Humane Society of the United States has put together a tip sheet for airline traveling. You can receive a copy by sending a self-addressed stamped envelope to:

Do not allow your Labrador to stick his head out of the window of a moving vehicle. Debris can easily fly into your Labrador's eyes.

The Humane Society of the United States
Tip Sheet

2100 L Street NW
Washington, DC 20037.

Regulations differ for traveling outside of the country and are sometimes changed without notice. Well in advance you need to write or call the appropriate consulate or agricultural department for instructions. Some countries have lengthy quarantines (six months), and countries differ in their rabies vaccination requirements. For instance, it may have to be given at least 30 days ahead of your departure.

Do make sure your dog is wearing proper identification. You never know when you might be in an accident and separated from your dog. Or your dog could be frightened and somehow manage to escape and run away. When I travel, my dogs wear collars with engraved nameplates with my name, phone

There are many good boarding facilities available. Ask your veterinarian or a dog-owning friend to recommend a reputable one.

number and city.

Another suggestion would be to carry in-case-of-emergency instructions. These would include the address and phone number of a relative or friend, your veterinarian's name, address and phone number, and your dog's medical information.

BOARDING KENNELS

Perhaps you have decided that you need to board your dog. Your veterinarian can recommend a good boarding facility or possibly a pet sitter that will come to your house. It is customary for the boarding kennel to ask for proof of vaccination for the DHLPP, rabies and bordetella vaccine. The bordetella should have been given within six months of boarding. This is for your protection. If they do not

A reputable boarding kennel will require that dogs receive the vaccination for kennel cough no less than two weeks before their scheduled stay.

ask for this proof I would not board at their kennel. Ask about flea control. Those dogs that suffer flea-bite allergy can get in trouble at a boarding kennel. Unfortunately boarding kennels are limited on how much they are able to do.

For more information on pet sitting, contact NAPPS: National Association of Professional Pet Sitters 1200 G Street, NW Suite 760 Washington, DC 20005.

Our clinic has technicians that pet sit and technicians that board clinic patients in their homes. This may be an alternative for you. Ask your veterinarian if they have an employee that can help you. There is a definite advantage of having a technician care for your dog, especially if your dog is on medication or is a senior citizen.

You can write for a copy of *Traveling With Your Pet* from ASPCA, Education Department, 441 E. 92nd Street, New York, NY 10128.

IDENTIFICATION and Finding the Lost Dog

There are several ways of identifying your dog. The old standby is a collar with dog license, rabies, and ID tags. Unfortunately collars have a way of being separated from the dog and tags fall off. I am not suggesting you shouldn't use a collar and tags. If they stay intact and on the dog, they are the quickest way of identification.

For several years owners have been tattooing their dogs. Some tattoos use a number with a registry. Here lies the problem because there are several registries to check. If you wish to

An identification tag placed on your Labrador's collar should carry your address and phone number in case he is ever lost. Owner, Connie Howard.

tattoo, use your social security number. The humane shelters have the means to trace it. It is usually done on the inside of the rear thigh. The area is first shaved and numbed. There is no pain, although a few dogs do not like the buzzing sound. Occasionally tattooing is not legible and needs to be redone.

The newest method of identification is microchipping. The microchip is a computer chip that is no larger than a grain of rice. The veterinarian implants it by injection between the shoulder blades. The dog feels no discomfort. If your dog is lost and picked up by the humane society, they can trace you by scanning the microchip, which has its own code. Microchip scanners are friendly to other brands of microchips and their registries. The microchip comes with a dog tag saying the dog is microchipped. It is the safest way of identifying your dog.

FINDING THE LOST DOG

I am sure you will agree with me that there would be little worse than losing your dog. Responsible pet owners rarely lose their dogs. They do not let their dogs run free because they don't want harm to come to them. Not only that but in most, if not all, states there is a leash law.

Beware of fenced-in yards. They can be a hazard. Dogs find ways to escape either over or under the fence. Another fast exit is through the gate that perhaps the neighbor's child left unlocked.

Below is a list that hopefully will be of help to you if you need it. Remember don't give up, keep looking. Your dog is worth your efforts.

1. Contact your neighbors and put flyers with a photo on it in their mailboxes. Information you should include would be the dog's name, breed, sex, color, age, source of identification, when your dog was last seen and where, and your name and phone numbers. It may be helpful to say the dog needs medical care. Offer a *reward*.

2. Check all local shelters daily. It is also possible for your dog to be picked up away from home and end up in an out-of-the-way shelter. Check these too. Go in person. It is not good enough to call. Most shelters are limited on the time they can hold dogs then they are put up

Microchipping is a new method for dog identification. The veterinarian can implant it by injection between the shoulder blades.

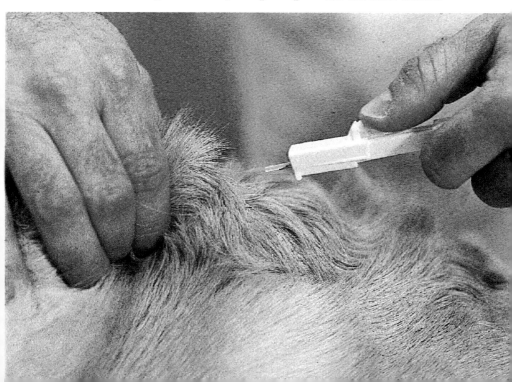

A properly secured collar will assure that your Labrador cannot slip away and run off. Check the collar periodically to ensure a proper fit.

for adoption or euthanized. There is the possibility that your dog will not make it to the shelter for several days. Your dog could have been wandering or someone may have tried to keep him.

3. Notify all local veterinarians. Call and send flyers.

4. Call your breeder. Frequently breeders are contacted when one of their breed is found.

5. Contact the rescue group for your breed.

6. Contact local schools—children may have seen your dog.

7. Post flyers at the schools, groceries, gas stations, convenience stores, veterinary clinics, groomers and any other place that will allow them.

8. Advertise in the newspaper.

9. Advertise on the radio.

DENTAL CARE for Your Dog's Life

So you've got a new puppy! You also have a new set of puppy teeth in your household. Anyone who has ever raised a puppy is abundantly aware of these new teeth. Your puppy will chew anything it can reach, chase your shoelaces, and play "tear the rag" with any piece of clothing it can find. When puppies are newly born, they have no teeth. At about four weeks of age, puppies of most breeds begin to develop their deciduous or baby teeth. They begin eating semi-solid food, fighting and biting with their litter mates, and learning discipline from their mother. As their new teeth come in, they inflict more pain on their mother's breasts, so her feeding sessions become less frequent and shorter. By six or eight weeks, the mother will start growling to warn her pups when they are fighting too roughly or hurting her as they nurse too much with their new teeth.

Puppies need to chew. It is a necessary part of their physical and mental development. They develop muscles and necessary life skills as they drag objects around, fight over possession, and vocalize alerts and warnings. Puppies chew on things to explore their world. They are using their sense of taste to determine what is food and what is not. How else can they tell an electrical cord from a lizard? At about four months of age, most puppies begin shedding their baby teeth. Often

Puppies need something to chew on during their teething period. Encourage constructive chewing by providing your Labrador Retriever pup with a Gumabone®.

these teeth need some help to come out and make way for the permanent teeth. The incisors (front teeth) will be replaced first. Then, the adult canine or fang teeth erupt. When the baby tooth is not shed before the permanent tooth comes in, veterinarians call it a retained deciduous

A chicken-flavored Gumabone® has tiny particles of chicken powder embedded in it to keep the Labrador interested.

tooth. This condition will often cause gum infections by trapping hair and debris between the permanent tooth and the retained baby tooth. Nylafloss® is an excellent device for puppies to use. They can toss it, drag it,

Labrador Retriever relaxing with his Gumabone®. These chew toys come in a variety of colors and shapes, and Labradors love to chew them.

and chew on the many surfaces it presents. The baby teeth can catch in the nylon material, aiding in their removal. Puppies that have adequate chew toys will have less destructive behavior, develop more physically, and have less chance of retained deciduous teeth.

During the first year, your dog should be seen by your veterinarian at regular intervals. Your veterinarian will let you know when to bring in your puppy for vaccinations and parasite examinations. At each visit, your veterinarian should inspect the lips, teeth, and mouth as part of a complete physical examination. You should take some part in the maintenance of your dog's oral health. You should examine your dog's mouth weekly throughout his first year to make sure there are no sores, foreign objects, tooth problems, etc. If your dog drools excessively, shakes its head, or has bad breath, consult your veterinarian. By the time your dog is six months old, the permanent teeth are all in and plaque can start to accumulate on the tooth surfaces. This is when your dog needs to develop good dental-care habits to prevent calculus build-up on its teeth. Brushing is best. That is a fact that cannot be denied. However, some dogs do not like their teeth brushed regularly, or you may not be able to accomplish the task. In that case, you should consider a product that will help prevent plaque and calculus build-up.

Nylabone® products are so much fun for your Labrador Retriever that he will never want to put them down. Owners, Jim and Debbie Gardner.

The Plaque Attackers® and Galileo Bone® are other excellent choices for the first three years of a dog's life. Their shapes make them interesting for the dog. As the dog chews on them, the solid polyurethane massages the gums which improves the blood circulation to the periodontal tissues. Projections on the chew devices increase the surface and are in contact with the tooth for more efficient cleaning. The unique shape and consistency prevent your dog from exerting excessive force on his own teeth or from breaking off pieces of the bone. If your dog is an aggressive chewer or weighs more than 55 pounds (25 kg), you should consider giving him a Nylabone®, the most durable chew product on the market.

Your Labrador Retriever will have many hours of entertainment with his Gumabone®.

The Gumabone®, made by the Nylabone Company, is constructed of strong polyurethane, which is softer than nylon. Less powerful chewers prefer the Gumabones® to the Nylabones®. A super option for your dog is the Hercules Bone®, a uniquely shaped bone named after the great Olympian for its exceptional strength. Like all Nylabone products, they are specially scented to make them attractive to your dog. Ask your veterinarian about these bones and he will validate the good doctor's prescription: Nylabones® not only give your dog a good chewing workout but also help to save your dog's teeth (and even his life, as it protects him from possible fatal periodontal diseases).

By the time dogs are four years old, 75% of them have periodontal disease. It is the most common infection in dogs. Yearly examinations by your veterinarian are essential to maintaining your dog's good health. If your veterinarian detects periodontal disease, he or she may recommend a prophylactic cleaning. To do a thorough cleaning, it will be necessary to put your dog under anesthesia. With modern gas anesthetics and monitoring equipment, the procedure is pretty safe. Your veterinarian will scale the teeth with an ultrasound scaler or hand instrument. This removes the calculus from the teeth. If there are calculus deposits below the gum line, the veterinarian will plane the roots to make them smooth. After all of the calculus has been removed, the teeth are polished with pumice in a polishing cup. If any medical or surgical treatment is needed, it is done at this time. The final step would be fluoride treatment and your follow-up treatment at home. If the periodontal disease is advanced, the veterinarian may prescribe a medicated mouth rinse or antibiotics for use at home. Make sure your dog has safe, clean and attractive chew toys and treats. Chooz® treats are another way of using a consumable treat to help keep your dog's teeth clean.

Rawhide is the most popular of all materials for a dog to chew. This has never been good news to dog owners, because rawhide is inherently very dangerous for dogs. Thousands of dogs have died from rawhide, having swallowed the hide after it has become soft and mushy, only to cause stomach and intestinal blockage. A new rawhide product on the market has finally solved the problem of rawhide: molded Roar-Hide®

from Nylabone. These are composed of processed, cut up, and melted American rawhide injected into your dog's favorite shape: a dog bone. These dog-safe devices smell and taste like rawhide but don't break up. The ridges on the bones help to fight tartar build-up on the teeth and they last ten times longer than the usual rawhide chews.

As your dog ages, professional examination and cleaning should become more frequent. The mouth should be inspected at least once a year. Your veterinarian may recommend visits every six months. In the geriatric patient, organs such as the heart, liver, and kidneys do not function as well as when they were young. Your veterinarian will probably want to test these organs' functions prior to using general anesthesia for dental cleaning. If your dog is a good chewer and you work closely with your veterinarian, your dog can

The Hercules™ from Nylabone® products, is made of polyurethane, like some car bumpers. It has been designed especially for Labradors and other powerful chewing breeds.

keep all of its teeth all of its life. However, as your dog ages, his sense of smell, sight, and taste will diminish. He may not have the desire to chase, trap or chew his toys. He will also not have the energy to chew for long periods, as arthritis and periodontal disease make chewing painful. This will leave you with more responsibility for keeping his teeth clean and healthy. The dog that would not let you brush his teeth at one year of age, may let you brush his teeth now that he is ten years old.

If you train your dog with good chewing habits as a puppy, he will have healthier teeth throughout his life.

HEALTH CARE for Your Labrador

Veterinary medicine has become far more sophisticated than what was available to our ancestors. This can be attributed to the increase in household pets and consequently the demand for better care for them. Also human medicine has become far more complex. Today diagnostic testing in veterinary medicine parallels human diagnostics. Because of better technology we can expect our pets to live healthier lives thereby increasing their life spans.

THE FIRST CHECK UP

You will want to take your new puppy/dog in for its first check up within 48 to 72 hours after acquiring it. Many breeders strongly recommend this check up and so do the humane shelters. A puppy/dog can appear healthy but it may have a serious problem that is not apparent to the layman. Most pets have some type of a minor flaw that may never cause a real problem.

Unfortunately if he/she should have a serious problem, you will want to consider the consequences of keeping the pet and the attachments that will be formed, which may be broken prematurely. Keep in mind there are many healthy dogs looking for good homes.

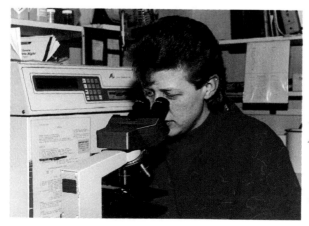

Laboratory tests are studied by highly trained veterinary technicians. Most tests are performed right in your own veterinarian's office.

This first check up is a good time to establish yourself with the veterinarian and learn the office policy regarding their hours and how they handle emergencies. Usually the breeder or another conscientious pet owner is a good reference for locating a capable veterinarian. You should be aware that not all veterinarians give the same quality of service. Please do not make your selection on the least expensive

Labradors are prone to heatstroke and should be kept cool on hot, sunny days.

Puppies receive maternal antibodies from their dam's milk. In cases of pups that are hand-reared, vaccinations are most imperative.

clinic, as they may be short changing your pet. There is the possibility that eventually it will cost you more due to improper diagnosis, treatment, etc. If you are selecting a new veterinarian, feel free to ask for a tour of the clinic. You should inquire about making an

appointment for a tour since all clinics are working clinics, and therefore may not be available all day for sightseers. You may worry less if you see where your pet will be spending the day if he ever needs to be hospitalized.

THE PHYSICAL EXAM

Your veterinarian will check your pet's overall condition, which includes listening to the heart; checking the respiration; feeling the abdomen, muscles and joints; checking the mouth, which includes the gum color and signs of gum disease along with plaque buildup; checking the ears for signs of an infection or ear mites; examining the eyes; and, last but not least, checking the condition of the skin and coat.

He should ask you questions regarding your pet's eating and elimination habits and invite you to relay your questions. It is a good idea to prepare a list so as not to forget anything. He should discuss the proper diet and the quantity to be fed. If this should differ from your breeder's recommendation, then you should convey to him the breeder's choice and see if he approves. If he recommends changing the diet, then this should be done over a few days so as not to cause a gastrointestinal upset. It is customary to take in a fresh stool sample (just a small amount) for a test for intestinal parasites. It must be fresh, preferably within 12 hours, since the eggs hatch quickly and after hatching will not be observed under the microscope. If your pet isn't obliging then, usually the technician can take one in the clinic.

IMMUNIZATIONS

It is important that you take your puppy/dog's vaccination record with you on your first visit. In case of a puppy, presumably the breeder has seen to the vaccinations up to the time you acquired custody. Veterinarians differ in their vaccination protocol. It is not unusual for your puppy to have received vaccinations for distemper, hepatitis, leptospirosis, parvovirus and parainfluenza every two to three weeks from the age of five or six weeks. Usually this is a combined injection and is typically called the DHLPP. The DHLPP is given through at least 12 to 14 weeks of age, and it is customary to continue with another parvovirus vaccine at 16 to 18 weeks. You may wonder why so many immunizations are necessary.

No one knows for sure when the puppy's maternal antibodies are gone, although it is customarily accepted that distemper antibodies are gone by 12 weeks. Usually parvovirus antibodies are gone by 16 to 18 weeks of age. However, it is possible for the maternal antibodies to be gone at a much earlier age or even a later age. Therefore immunizations are started at an early age. The vaccine will not give immunity as long as there are maternal antibodies.

The rabies vaccination is given at three or six months of age depending on your local laws. A vaccine for bordetella (kennel cough) is advisable and can be given anytime from the age of five weeks. The coronavirus is not commonly given unless there is a problem locally. The Lyme vaccine is necessary in endemic areas. Lyme disease has been reported in 47 states.

Distemper

This is virtually an incurable disease. If the dog recovers, he is subject to severe nervous disorders. The virus attacks every tissue in the body and resembles a bad cold with a fever. It can cause a runny nose and eyes and cause gastrointestinal disorders, including a poor appetite, vomiting and diarrhea. The virus is carried by raccoons,

The health of your Labrador will show in his overall appearance and attitude.

foxes, wolves, mink and other dogs. Unvaccinated youngsters and senior citizens are very susceptible. This is still a common disease.

Hepatitis

This is a virus that is most serious in very young dogs. It is spread by contact with an infected animal or its stool or urine. The virus affects the liver and kidneys and is characterized by high fever, depression and lack of appetite. Recovered animals may be afflicted with chronic illnesses.

Leptospirosis

This is a bacterial disease transmitted by contact with the urine of an infected dog, rat or other wildlife. It produces severe symptoms of fever, depression, jaundice and internal bleeding and was fatal before the vaccine was developed. Recovered dogs can be carriers, and the disease can be transmitted from dogs to humans.

Parvovirus

This was first noted in the late 1970s and is still a fatal disease. However, with proper vaccinations, early diagnosis and prompt treatment, it is a manageable disease. It attacks the heart, bone marrow and intestinal tract. The symptoms include depression, loss of appetite, vomiting, diarrhea and collapse. Immediate medical attention is of the essence.

Rabies

This is shed in the saliva and is carried by raccoons, skunks, foxes, other dogs and cats. It attacks nerve tissue, resulting in paralysis and death. Rabies can be transmitted to people and is virtually always fatal. This disease is reappearing in the suburbs.

Bordetella (Kennel Cough)

The symptoms are coughing, sneezing, hacking and retching accompanied by nasal discharge usually lasting from a few days

Kennel cough is a highly contagious disease, and a vaccination always should be given to dogs that come in contact with other dogs.

to several weeks. There are several disease-producing organisms responsible for this disease. The present vaccines are helpful but do not protect for all the strains. It usually is not life threatening but in some instances it can progress to a serious bronchopneumonia. The disease is highly contagious. The vaccination should be given routinely for dogs that come in contact with other dogs, such as through boarding, training class or visits to the groomer.

Bordetella attached to canine cilia. This disease is not life-threatening but can progress to a serious bronchopneumonia.

Coronavirus

This is usually self limiting and not life threatening. It was first noted in the late '70s about a year before parvovirus. The virus produces a yellow/brown stool and there may be depression, vomiting and diarrhea.

Lyme Disease

This was first diagnosed in the United States in 1976 in Lyme, CT in people who lived in close proximity to the deer tick. Symptoms may include acute lameness, fever, swelling of joints and loss of appetite. Your veterinarian can advise you if you live in an endemic area.

After your puppy has completed his puppy vaccinations, you will continue to booster the DHLPP once a year. It is customary to booster the rabies one year after the first vaccine and then, depending on where you live, it should be boostered every year or every three years. This depends on your local laws. The Lyme and corona vaccines are boostered annually and it is recommended that the bordetella be boostered every six to eight months.

Annual Visit

I would like to impress the importance of the annual check up, which would include the booster vaccinations, check for intestinal parasites and test for heartworm. Today in our very busy world it is rush, rush and see "how much you can get for how little." Unbelievably, some non-veterinary businesses have entered into the vaccination business. More harm than good can come to your dog through improper vaccinations, possibly from inferior vaccines and/or the wrong schedule. More than likely you truly care about your companion dog and over the years you have devoted much time and expense to his well being. Perhaps you are unaware that a vaccination is not just a vaccination. There is more involved. Please, please follow through with regular physical examinations. It is so important for your veterinarian to know your dog and this is especially true during middle age through the geriatric years. More than likely your older dog will require more than one physical a year. The annual physical is good preventive medicine. Through early diagnosis and subsequent treatment your dog can maintain a longer and better quality of life.

INTESTINAL PARASITES

Hookworms

These are an almost microscopic intestinal worms that can cause anemia and therefore serious problems, including death, in young puppies. Hookworms can be transmitted to humans through penetration of the skin. Puppies may be born with them.

Roundworms

These are spaghetti-like worms that can cause a potbellied appearance and dull coat along with more severe symptoms, such as vomiting, diarrhea and coughing. Puppies acquire these while in the mother's uterus and through lactation. Both hookworms and roundworms may be acquired through ingestion.

Whipworms

These have a three-month life cycle and are not acquired through the dam. They cause intermittent diarrhea usually with mucus. Whipworms are possibly the most difficult worm to eradicate. Their eggs are very resistant to most environmental factors and can last for years until the proper conditions enable them to mature. Whipworms are seldom seen in the stool.

Intestinal parasites are more prevalent in some areas than

others. Climate, soil and contamination are big factors contributing to the incidence of intestinal parasites. Eggs are passed in the stool, lay on the ground and then become infective in a certain number of days. Each of the above worms has a different life cycle. Your best chance of becoming and remaining worm-free is to always pooper-scoop your yard. A fenced-in yard keeps stray dogs out, which is certainly helpful.

I would recommend having a fecal examination on your dog twice a year or more often if there is a problem. If your dog has a positive fecal sample, then he will be given the appropriate medication and you will be asked to bring back another stool sample in a certain period of time (depending on the type of worm) and then be rewormed. This process goes on until he has at least two negative samples. The different types of worms require different medications. You will be wasting your money and doing your dog an injustice by buying over-the-counter medication without first consulting your veterinarian.

Before you socialize your Labrador Retriever puppy, make sure both dogs have up-to-date inoculations.

OTHER INTERNAL PARASITES

Coccidiosis and Giardiasis

These protozoal infections usually affect puppies, especially in places where large numbers of puppies are brought together. Older dogs may harbor these infections but do not show signs unless they are stressed. Symptoms include diarrhea, weight loss and lack of appetite. These infections are not always apparent in the fecal examination.

Tapeworms

Seldom apparent on fecal floatation, they are diagnosed frequently as rice-like segments around the dog's anus and the base of the tail. Tapeworms are long, flat and ribbon like, sometimes several feet in length, and made up of many segments about five-eighths of an inch long. The two most common types of tapeworms found in the dog are:

(1) First the larval form of the flea tapeworm parasite must mature in an intermediate host, the flea, before it can become infective. Your dog acquires this by ingesting the flea through licking and chewing.

(2) Rabbits, rodents and certain large game animals serve as intermediate hosts for other species of tapeworms. If your dog should eat one of these infected hosts, then he can acquire tapeworms.

HEARTWORM DISEASE

This is a worm that resides in the heart and adjacent blood vessels of the lung that produces microfilaria, which circulate in the bloodstream. It is possible for a dog to be infected with any number of worms from one to a hundred that can be 6 to 14 inches long. It is a life-threatening disease, expensive to treat and easily prevented.

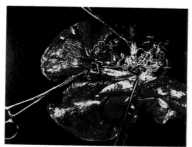

Dirofilaria—adult worms in heart of a dog. It is possible for a dog to be infected with any number of worms from one to a hundred. Courtesy of Merck Ag Vet.

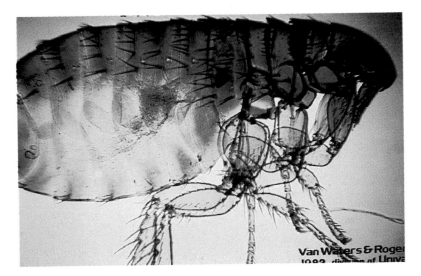

The cat flea is the most common flea of both dogs and cats. Courtesy of Fleabusters, Rx for Fleas, Inc., Ft. Lauderdale, Florida.

Depending on where you live, your veterinarian may recommend a preventive year-round and either an annual or semiannual blood test. The most common preventive is given once a month.

EXTERNAL PARASITES

Fleas

These pests are not only the dog's worst enemy but also enemy to the owner's pocketbook. Preventing is less expensive than treating, but regardless I think we'd prefer to spend our money elsewhere. I would guess that the majority of our dogs are allergic to the bite of a flea, and in many cases it only takes one flea bite. The protein in the flea's saliva is the culprit. Allergic dogs have a reaction, which usually results in a "hot spot." More than likely such a reaction will involve a trip to the veterinarian for treatment. Yes, prevention is less expensive. Fortunately today there are several good products available.

If there is a flea infestation, no one product is going to correct the problem. Not only will the dog require treatment so will the environment. In general flea collars are not very

Fleas are easily picked up in heavily grassed areas. Groom your Labrador Retriever after an outing in a field to reduce the chance of a flea problem.

effective although there is now available an "egg" collar that will kill the eggs on the dog. Dips are the most economical but they are messy. There are some effective shampoos and treatments available through pet shops and veterinarians. An oral tablet arrived on the American market in 1995 and was popular in Europe the previous year. It sterilizes the female flea but will not kill adult fleas. Therefore the tablet, which is given monthly, will decrease the flea population but is not a "cure-all." Those dogs that suffer from flea-bite allergy will still be subjected to the bite of the flea. Another popular parasiticide is permethrin, which is applied to the back of the dog in one or two places depending on the dog's weight. This product works as a repellent causing the flea to get "hot feet" and jump off. Do not confuse this product with some of the organophosphates that are also applied to the dog's back.

Some products are not usable on young puppies. Treating

fleas should be done under your veterinarian's guidance. Frequently it is necessary to combine products and the layman does not have the knowledge regarding possible toxicities. It is hard to believe but there are a few dogs that do have a natural resistance to fleas. Nevertheless it would be wise to treat all pets at the same time. Don't forget your cats. Cats just love to prowl the neighborhood and consequently return with unwanted guests.

Adult fleas live on the dog but their eggs drop off the dog into the environment. There they go through four larval stages before reaching adulthood, and thereby are able to jump back on the poor unsuspecting dog. The cycle resumes and takes between 21 to 28 days under ideal conditions. There are environmental products available that will kill both the adult fleas and the larvae.

To prevent and eliminate flea infestation use a safe insecticide to kill adult fleas in the house and an insect growth regulator to stop the eggs and larvae in the environment.

Ticks

Ticks carry Rocky Mountain Spotted Fever, Lyme disease and can cause tick paralysis. They should be removed with tweezers, trying to pull out the head. The jaws carry disease. There is a tick preventive collar that does an excellent job. The ticks automatically back out on those dogs wearing collars.

Sarcoptic Mange

This is a mite that is difficult to find on skin scrapings. The pinnal reflex is a good indicator of this disease. Rub the ends of the pinna (ear) together and the dog will start scratching with his foot. Sarcoptes are highly contagious to other dogs and to humans although they do not live long on humans. They cause intense itching.

Demodectic Mange

This is a mite that is passed from the dam to her puppies. It affects youngsters age three to ten months. Diagnosis is confirmed by skin scraping. Small areas of alopecia around the eyes, lips and/or forelegs become visible. There is little itching unless there is a secondary bacterial infection. Some breeds are afflicted more than others.

Cheyletiella

This causes intense itching and is diagnosed by skin scraping. It lives in the outer layers of the skin of dogs, cats, rabbits and humans. Yellow-gray scales may be found on the back and the rump, top of the head and the nose.

TO BREED OR NOT TO BREED

More than likely your breeder has requested that you have your puppy neutered or spayed. Your breeder's request is based on what is healthiest for your dog and what is most beneficial for your breed. Experienced and conscientious breeders devote many years into developing a bloodline. In order to do this, he makes every effort to plan each breeding in regard to conformation,

The demodex mite is passed from the dam to her puppies. It affects youngsters from the ages of three to ten months.

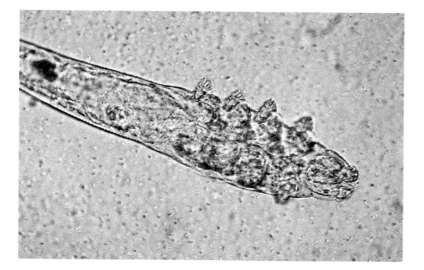

Labrador breeders are highly selective in their pairings. Breeding should be left to the experts to ensure the betterment of the breed.

temperament and health. This type of breeder does his best to perform the necessary testing (i.e., OFA, CERF, testing for inherited blood disorders, thyroid, etc.). Testing is expensive and sometimes very disheartening when a favorite dog doesn't pass his health tests. The health history pertains not only to the breeding stock but to the immediate ancestors. Reputable breeders do not want their offspring to be bred indiscriminately. Therefore you may be asked to neuter or spay your puppy. Of course there is always the exception, and your breeder may agree to let you breed your dog under his direct supervision. This is an important concept. More and more effort is being made to breed healthier dogs.

Spay/Neuter

There are numerous benefits of performing this surgery at six months of age. An unspayed female is subject to mammary and ovarian cancer. In order to prevent mammary cancer she must be spayed prior to her first heat cycle. Later in life, an unspayed female may develop a pyometra (an infected uterus), which is definitely life threatening.

Spaying is performed under a general anesthetic and is easy on the young dog. As you might expect it is a little harder on the older dog, but that is no reason to deny her the surgery. The surgery removes the ovaries and uterus. It is important to remove all the ovarian tissue. If some is left behind, she could remain attractive to males. In order to view the ovaries, a reasonably long incision is necessary. An ovariohysterectomy is considered major surgery.

Neutering the male at a young age will inhibit some characteristic male behavior that owners frown upon. I have found my boys will not hike their legs and mark territory if they are neutered at six months of age. Also neutering at a young age has hormonal benefits, lessening the chance of hormonal aggressiveness.

Surgery involves removing the testicles but leaving the scrotum. If there should be a retained testicle, then he definitely needs to be neutered before the age of two or three years. Retained testicles can develop into cancer. Unneutered males are at risk for testicular cancer, perineal fistulas, perianal tumors and fistulas and prostatic disease.

Intact males and females are prone to housebreaking accidents. Females urinate frequently before, during and after heat cycles, and males tend to mark territory if there is a female in heat. Males may show the same behavior if there is a visiting dog or guests.

Surgery involves a sterile operating procedure equivalent to human surgery. The incision site is shaved, surgically scrubbed and draped. The veterinarian wears a sterile surgical gown, cap, mask and gloves. Anesthesia should be monitored by a registered technician. It is customary for the veterinarian to recommend a pre-anesthetic blood screening, looking for

Some male Labradors may exhibit hormonal aggressiveness. The chance of this can be lessened by neutering at a young age.

metabolic problems and a ECG rhythm strip to check for normal heart function. Today anesthetics are equal to human anesthetics, which enables your dog to walk out of the clinic the same day as surgery.

Showing your Labrador can be the most fun and rewarding experience that you have ever had.

Some folks worry about their dog's gaining weight after being neutered or spayed. This is usually not the case. It is true that some dogs may be less active so they could develop a problem, but my own dogs are just as active as they were before surgery. I have a hard time keeping weight on them. However, if your dog should begin to gain, then you need to decrease his food and see to it that he gets a little more exercise.

Newborn puppies are a big responsibility. This is a three-week-old female puppy.

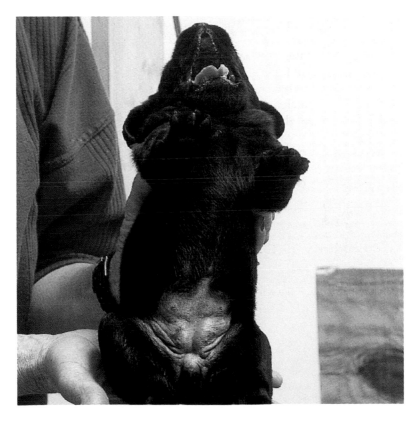

SUGGESTED READING

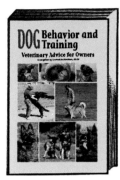

TS-252
Dog Behavior and
Training
288 pages, nearly
200 color photos.

TS-249
Skin & Coat Care
for Your Dog
224 pages, 300
color photos.

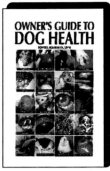

TS-214
Owner's Guide to
Dog Health
432 pages, 300
color photos.

TS-205
Successful
Dog
Training
160 pages,
130 color
photos.

TS-258
Training Your
Dog For Sports
and Other
Activities
160 pages, over
200 color photos.

TW-140
The Proper Care of
Labrador Retrievers
256 pages, over 200
full-color photos.

H-1059
Book of the
Labrador Retriever
478 pages, over 100
full color photos.

TS-241
The Official Book of
the Labrador
Retriever
416 pages, full color
photos throughout.

INDEX